COACHING THROUGH SUPERIORITIES

Tactical Problem-Solving in Football

Ray Power

BENNION KEARNY

Published in 2025 by Bennion Kearny Limited.

Copyright © Bennion Kearny Limited 2025

Ray Power has asserted his right under the Copyright, Designs and Patents Act, 1988 to be identified as the author of this book.

ISBN: 9781915855367

All Rights Reserved. No part of this publication may be reproduced, stored in a retrieval system, or transmitted in any form or by any means, electronic, mechanical, photocopying, recording or otherwise, without the prior permission of the publisher.

This book is sold subject to the condition that it shall not, by way of trade or otherwise, be lent, re-sold, hired out or otherwise circulated without the publisher's prior consent in any form of binding or cover other than that in which it is published and without a similar condition including this condition being imposed on the subsequent purchaser.

Bennion Kearny has endeavoured to provide trademark information about all the companies and products mentioned in this book by the appropriate use of capitals. However, Bennion Kearny cannot guarantee the accuracy of this information.

Published by Bennion Kearny Limited
6 Woodside
Churnet View Road
Oakamoor
ST10 3AE

www.BennionKearny.com

About Ray Power

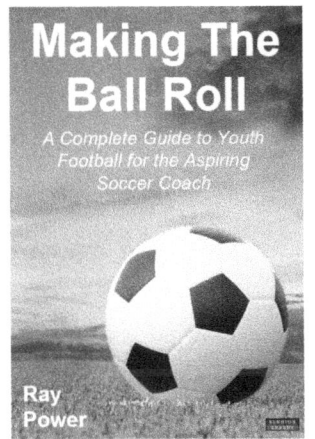

Ray Power is one of the bestselling football authors in the world.

With almost two decades of experience working in football and education, coaching players from non-league to Premier League levels, and internationally, he is the author of *Making the Ball Roll*, *Coaching Youth Football*, and the five-book *Deliberate Soccer Practice* series.

As a coach developer and educator, Ray has worked for, and consulted with, numerous national FAs, as well as governing bodies from other sports, including the NBA.

He also works as a consultant – mentor – educator on a freelance basis, working with grassroots coaches all the way to professional teams.

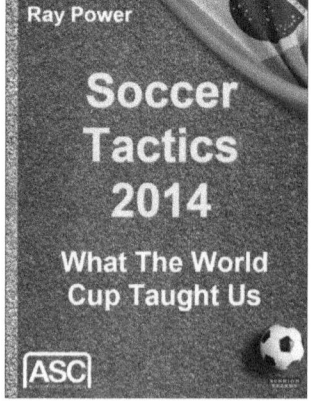

Table of Contents

Foreword 1
Imbued with Football 1
Superiorities 2
Attracted by Dynamism 3

Introduction: Understanding You & Tactics 5
Understanding Football Tactics 6
Tactics: Four Corners, Four Moments & Decision-Making 7
    The Four Moments of the Game 9
    Decision-Making BOTS 13
    State of the Game 15
Baseline Tactics 17
    Your Style 17
Football Formations 20
    Your Base Formation 23
    Players Change How Formations Function 25
Conclusion 27
    Moving Forward Through Superiorities 28

Introducing Superiorities (Simply!) 29
Superiorities 29
    Five Superiorities 29

Numerical Superiority (We Have More Players Than You) 33
A Game of 1v0 – 11v11 34

  A Game of 1v1s (1v0) 37
  A Game of Smaller Games? 42
  The Game as 11v11 43
Dynamic Numerical Superiority 47
  Out of Possession Dynamic Numerical Superiority 48
   Opposition's Half 48
   Our Half 49
  In Possession Dynamic Numerical Superiority 49
   First Third ('Build-Up') 49
   Middle Third ('Progress & Penetrate the Ball') 50
   Final Third ('Create & Score') 51
  Transitional Dynamic Numerical Superiority 52
   Transition to Defend (Losing the Ball) 52
   Transition to Attack (Winning the Ball) 53
Conclusion 54

Qualitative Superiority (We Have Better Players Than You) 55
Understanding 'Better' 56
  Messi? Ronaldo? 56
  Comparing Footballers – Apples and Oranges 57
  Attributes 61
1v1 64
  Not all 1v1s are the Same 66
  Being Superior 1v1 Defensively Wins Games Too 67
  Goalkeepers 67
  Capitalising on Weaknesses 68
Units & Teams 69
Conclusion 74

Positional Superiority (Our Players are Better Positioned Than Yours) 77

Pitch Control 79

In Possession – The Most Advantageous Spaces 81

    The Golden Zone 83

    Zone 14 84

    The Halfspaces 86

    The Wide Channels Inside the Penalty Area 88

Dynamic Spaces 90

    Behind the Defence 91

    Playing Between and Behind the Lines 92

    Between Defenders 93

Individual Positional Superiority 94

    Scanning – Awareness 95

    Body Orientation 95

    Individual Off-the-Ball Movement 96

    Press Resistance and Ball Retention 96

    Playing Under Pressure 96

Conclusion 97

Cooperative Superiority (Our Players are Better Together Than Yours) 99

Tactical Communication 100

    Playing Your Best Team 101

    Partnerships 102

    Units 105

    The Whole Team Function 108

        Team Cooperation – Out of Possession 110

    Substitutes and Using Your Squad 116

Conclusion – Dynamic Cooperative Superiority 121

Being Better (Other Superiorities) 123
Dynamic Superiority 123
From Individual to Group Dynamism 127
    Positional Play and Relationism 127
    Defending & Transitions 130
    Transitions 131
Dynamic Pauses 132
More Ways to Be Better 133
    Temporal Superiority 133
    Psychological Superiority 133
    Structural Superiority 134
    Conditional / Situational Superiority 134
    Refereeing Superiority 134
Conclusion 135

Conclusion (Review & Final Task) 135
    Numerical Superiority: More Than Just the Numbers 138
    Qualitative Superiority: Better Players, Better Choices 138
    Positional Superiority: Right Place, Right Time 138
    Cooperative Superiority: Better Together 139
    Dynamic Superiority: The Master Superiority 139
Conclusion 140

Foreword
Lee Johnson

Just a matter of weeks ago, I boarded a plane for Belgium to become the interim Head Coach of Lommel SK in the Belgian Challenger Pro League. In the days leading up to the flight, and on the journey itself, I, like many other coaches, and just like I did when I started new coaching roles in the UK, started with one question: *What's our edge?* Or, more accurately, what can be our edge? How can we find tactical advantages with our players that will help us win?

In the ever-evolving world of football, the quest for tactical advantages is relentless. As a manager who has navigated the challenges of various leagues and teams, I have come to appreciate the nuances that define success on the pitch.

Imbued with Football

I've lived and breathed football for as long as I can remember. In fact, I genuinely cannot remember too many days over the past 40+ years that the game of football has not been involved in my day-to-day activities. Growing up in a footballing household, I was immersed in the game from the very start. Some of my earliest memories involve travelling to training grounds and watching matches with a coach's eye, long before I fully understood what I was looking at.

I started out as a young player at Arsenal's academy, which set a high standard early on. From there, I spent time with Watford and Brighton, but it was at Yeovil Town where my professional playing career really came into focus. It was there where I first played an integral role in a squad as we pushed up through the leagues. I went on to play for Hearts in Scotland, and later Bristol City, among others. As a midfielder, I wasn't the flashiest on the pitch, but I prided myself on intelligence, work rate, and doing the unseen things that help a team tick.

With this immersion in football from the day I was old enough to roll a small ball around the family lounge, management eventually came naturally to me once I had stopped playing. It was always the long-term plan. I took my first steps into coaching and quickly got the opportunity to manage Oldham Athletic. At the time, I was the youngest manager in the Football League, and while that came with pressure, it also sharpened my edge early. From there, I've managed Barnsley, Bristol City, Sunderland, Hibernian, and in Belgium. Each role has shaped me differently, but the thread running through all of it has been a desire to coach in a way that challenges players to think, to problem-solve, and to understand the game on a deeper level. Football has never been just a job for me – it's a craft. And I see coaching as a lifelong apprenticeship.

Superiorities

It was in the search to refine my coaching craft that I came across Ray Power and his work, initially through some shared social media content, and then his coach education work and his coaching books. So, the opportunity to get on board with *Coaching Through Superiorities* was both a pleasure and an opportunity to deep dive the concepts.

In the following chapters, Ray delves into the five key superiorities and – as many of Ray's readers will know – he does so in plain English, making complex ideas understandable for all coaches.

I don't know exactly when I first came across the term "superiority" used in its current guise. And I am pretty sure my first deep dive into the subject left me dissatisfied with much of the convoluted material online that came back my way. It was almost like those writing about the topic were trying to make it sound more complicated!

Back when I played, we would certainly talk about out-numbering teams or a winger being better than the full-back. We'd talk about positioning, movement and, of course, working together.

It's Ray's comprehensive analysis of the five superiorities – Numerical, Qualitative, Positional, Cooperative, and Dynamic – however, that brings all this together to provide coaches with a framework to understand and implement these concepts effectively.

Attracted by Dynamism

One aspect of the book that resonates with me is the emphasis on dynamic superiority. One of the things that fellow coaches ask me about most often are my ideas around positional fluidity, so this won't be a surprise to those who know how I like my teams to play.

The modern game demands players who are not only technically proficient but also capable of making intelligent decisions under pressure. Ray's insights into developing this aspect of play are invaluable for coaches aiming to elevate their team's performance.

Moreover, the practical exercises and scenarios presented in the book offer coaches tangible methods to instil these principles within their squads. As someone who values the integration of technology and innovative training methods, I appreciate the book's approach to marrying theory with practice.

Ray's dedication to advancing coaching methodologies is evident throughout this work. His ability to distil complex tactical concepts into accessible strategies makes this book a must-read for coaches at all levels.

Coaching Through Superiorities is more than just a tactical manual; it's a roadmap for coaches striving to gain a competitive edge. Ray's insights will undoubtedly influence the next generation of football thinkers, and I, for one, look forward to applying these principles in my own coaching journey.

Enjoy the read and the exploration!

Lee Johnson

Introduction
Understanding You & Tactics

This book's premise is to inform and challenge *your* tactical thinking. It is, essentially, an opportunity to both learn about tactics and, significantly, to mentally prepare and rehearse game situations that will arise in your coaching future. It may also allow you to reflect and rethink previous tactical situations you and your team found yourselves in, and thus be better equipped to deal with these the next time they occur (and they will!).

TACTICAL TASK

At intervals throughout this book, you will come across these *Tactical Tasks.* There are two ways to approach them – you can:

Pause reading the book and complete the task immediately. Or complete the chapter, then complete the task(s)

Everyone is different. If I were completing these tasks, I would do so at the end of the chapter as a personal preference. There will be an advantage as later information can (and will) affect your previous answers.

Alternatively, completing the task immediately then re-completing it again (later on) has learning merit. You will have tackled and then re-tackled a problem, deepening the inherent learning.

I cannot tell you the number of tactical lightbulb moments I have had about a game – after the game! Sometimes, *way* after the final whistle! Whilst I used to kick myself for not figuring them out live, I realised that the next time something similar occurred, I had become better equipped to figure them out in the live arena. Do not underestimate the power of mental rehearsal and solving potential football problems before they even occur.

Bestselling author Simon Sinek advocates that everything we do should *start with why*. This book exists because I needed it years ago – and still need it now. It is a resource I wish I had earlier in my journey that would have helped me to practise and prepare for tactical situations *before they happened* – essentially tactical training for coaches. A place to safely fire the neurons in the brain before facing them in real life.

I suppose the first and broadest learning outcome from this book ought to be the acknowledgement *that all coaches will be, in some way or other, tactically deficient*. Whilst this may seem counter-intuitive, this realisation will actually set you free. Even deep into the 21st century, football is often a macho environment where the second you are named a coach – at whatever level – the expectation, actual or perceived, is that you should know everything. The truth, however, is that even the greatest coaches alive spend their days (and nights) searching for a solution to *that* problem. You see experts in our field get it wrong all the time. How many times have you seen Pep Guardiola scratch his head in thought?

For us mere mortals, it is therefore essential to embrace this process, enjoy learning, and ultimately move our tactical understanding needle forward from where it is now. Embrace the not-knowing.

Understanding Football Tactics

Before we delve into this problem-solving journey, a grounding in the realities of football tactics is necessary. The minute nuances of the game of football are so great that no book, coaching course, or YouTube video can comprehensively figure it *all* out. Such is the variability of football that even things that should look the same often don't. We talk mainly about patterns and principles but rarely absolute truths.

Some teams can look familiar in terms of formation, and the repetition of ideas in and out of possession (or when in transition)[1], but the outcomes can

---

[1] The *Four 'Moments' of the Game*.

be totally different. How Carlo Ancelotti and Sean Dyche approach the use of the GK:4-4-2 formation will be very different, although the 'shape' of the on-screen lineup will look the same, for example.

Whilst running a coaching course, I was once asked a question that stumped me, both because I didn't have an answer *and* because I was surprised it was asked at all: 'What is the best formation to use when the opponent is better'? All the eyes in the room fell on me, expecting a *definitive* answer – but they were not going to get one.

The most accurate answer to this question is both 'all of them' and 'none of them'! Actually, the most common answer to most closed tactical questions will be: "It depends". (Be prepared for a lot of "what ifs" and "it depends" as you journey through tactical understanding.) Football is far more complicated than single, straightforward answers. You can win or lose, or be better or worse in many different ways and as a result of many combinations. If it was as simple as one formation being somehow better than another, then we would never need to play a game again!

For every tactic, there is a counter-tactic. For every time you say that building from the back is best, someone will show you a clip of a cheap goal being conceded because of the ball being lost in build-up. For every deep defensive block, there is something that can unlock it. There are no purely correct, 100% right, successful tactics. And, even if there were, you are one individual error, one piece of magic, one refereeing decision, or one of hundreds of other micro-factors away from losing anyway.

Tactics: Four Corners, Four Moments & Decision-Making

In football – and player development especially – we often talk about the *Four Corners of the Game* (or *Long Term Player Development Model*), as below. Whilst some see this model as somewhat reductionist, it remains useful when we want to zoom in and focus on certain topics.

Long Term Player Development (LTPD) Model Widely used across soccer and sport	
Technical Tactical	Psychological
Physical	Social

Whilst we see and break football up into these distinct corners, we actually find that players and teams, as living organisms, become a melting pot of these corners – all operating and interacting together to produce an outcome. These four corners, and indeed characteristics from within each corner, bleed and blend together when we discuss players and the game.

For example, a *confident* (psychology) player takes on that *long-range shot* (technical-tactical) if she has the *power* to (physical) and feels the *support* from her teammates (social). A *quick* winger (physical) may take players on *1v1* if he has space to run into (technical-tactical), if his teammates *trust* him (social), and the player has *belief* in himself (psychological), even if he fails from time to time.

The *Technical-Tactical* corner, like the others, can be further sub-divided (not separated from) into its two obvious parts:

'Technical' – being the individual actions of a player with or around the ball.

'Tactical' – being their strategic actions on the pitch. This could be from individuals, units of players, or the team as a whole.

Let's be very clear, however: you can *zoom in* on certain technical or tactical aspects of the game, but you can never and should never completely *isolate* them from each other. Every individual technical action will manifest itself in a tactical way, just like moving a pawn in chess could be seen as one isolated move, whereas it is, in fact, contributing to the overall tactical chess match – attack one king, protect the other.

Each technical action contributes to a tactical outcome, and each tactical outcome needs technique. In football, each action will be to attack one goal or defend another one (or both).[2] For example, if your attacking strategy is to build through the thirds of the pitch, you will need technically proficient passing and receiving players (as well as dribblers) relative to the level of the game they are playing.[3] If it is to defend high up the pitch near the opponent's goal, defensive techniques like pressing, marking, jockeying, tracking, etc, are a necessity. We can *talk* about technique and tactics separately, but we cannot separate them.

The Four Moments of the Game

Here, we can further subdivide the tactical game into four distinct, but again, interlocking elements. Every team in every football game ever played is involved in a cycle between attacking and defending (some prefer to call this being 'In Possession' and 'Out of Possession') and then the transition moments which moderate them.

---

[2] Players in the highest leagues are now often signed based on data that quantifies whether their minute individual actions contribute to goals, or the creation of goal-scoring chances.

[3] A technically strong Premier League player is different to a technically strong local A-league under-12 player; a technically 'exceptional' player in Division Four may be completely technically deficient in the Premier League.

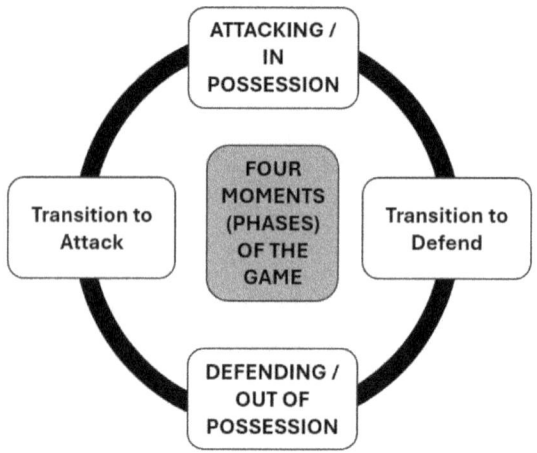

The Four Moments of the Game (Sometimes called Four Phases of the Game)

Coaches and players need to have a sense of how their team will play in these distinct moments, and that will be the challenge presented to you in the coming Task. You will often see this described as a 'Game Model'.

We can dissect these moments into further sections. The England DNA model, devised by the English FA, breaks these moments down as follows:[4]

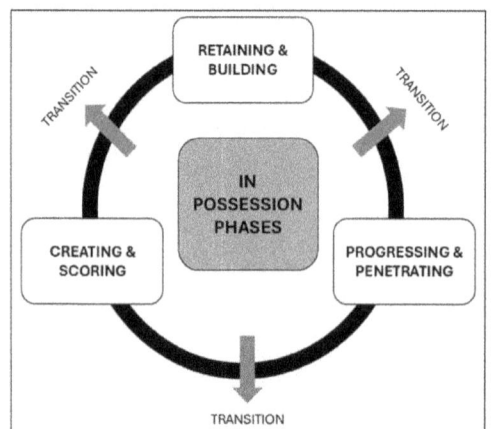 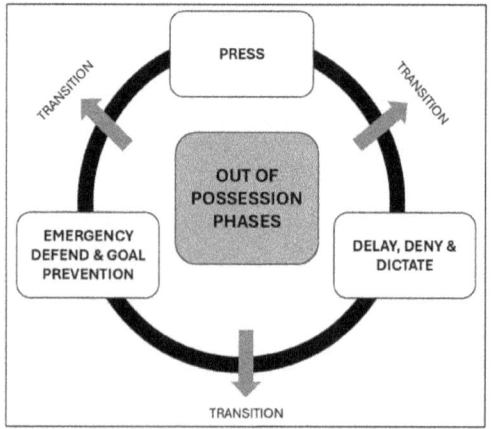

Breaking down In Possession & Out of Possession Phases: An adaptation of England DNA How We Play Model.

---

[4] I used some artistic licence and removed 'counter-attack' as an *In Possession* phase. This can be covered more clinically when looking at *Transition to Attack* phase.

TACTICAL TASKS 1 & 2

There are two ways in which coaches approach the building of their Game Model, which is essentially the team ideas in each of the Four Moments of the Game.

1. **DEFINE YOUR TEAM'S APPROACH ACROSS THESE FOUR PHASES, USING A MAXIMUM OF ONE OR TWO SENTENCES** (Post-It Note Approach).

2. **DEFINE YOUR TEAM'S APPROACH ACROSS THESE FOUR PHASES, USING AS MUCH DETAIL AS YOU POSSIBLY CAN. NOT ONLY BREAK DOWN EACH PHASE BUT BREAK DOWN EACH SUB-PHASE TOO** (Long Form Approach).

(You may actually find that both tasks above actually help you complete the other.)

Incidentally, set-pieces are considered the "fifth moment of the game" due to their uniqueness in football. No other moment in the game will involve a 'dead ball' and the opportunity to organise a routine or set of principles around a corner kick, free-kick, throw-in, goal-kick, or kick-off. Set-pieces, of course, can be for or against, and will contain transition moments, too.

Coaches can spend a lot of time putting together set-piece plans and routines, and you will notice now that a lot more specialist set-piece coaches work with professional teams. Previously, this was mainly seen in other sports, usually American ones, where data was more ingrained in the sport, including sports like Basketball and American Football, which involved more 'dead ball' restart moments.

It does make a huge amount of sense to take set-pieces very seriously. In a course completed with Stuart Reid, in association with the Association of Professional Football Analysis, it was found that set-pieces were the source of around 30% of goals and the equivalent of a 15-goal-a-season scorer in the English Premier League. Effectively employing set-pieces and defending them is a necessity.

TACTICAL TASK 3

OUTLINE YOUR APPROACH TO THE FOLLOWING SET-PIECES, BOTH FOR AND AGAINST:

- Corner-Kicks
- Free-Kicks (to shoot; to cross; to build-up)
- Throw-Ins
- Goal-Kicks
- Kick-Off
- Penalties (Penalty Shoot-Out?)

Decision-Making BOTS

What ties both technical actions and tactical outcomes together then is decision-making. A midfielder playing through the thirds must decide how, when, and where to pass or support the ball, what technique to use when passing from A to B, or whether to turn B down and pass to C, for example. A forward defending from the front must decide if to press, when to press, what passing lane to restrict, etc.

To understand tactics, we must understand the decision-making that informs technique. We must understand BOTS.

Unfortunately, when you type football or soccer 'BOTS' into an internet search engine, you end up in a rabbit hole of for-sale robotic products that somehow link to football. When it comes to coaching and understanding the game, however, the term BOTS has nothing to do with AI or robotics but serves as an acronym for the *four reference points* that players will use to make decisions on a football pitch.

The existence of these reference points cannot be understated. Every decision made on the field of play will relate to all four of these reference points.

BOTS	Example
Ball	The ball is the major reference point on the field of play. It is the toy that everyone wants to play with! This is why kids will swarm around it and why TV cameras follow it. What happens to the ball is more important than what happens to anything else on the field of play, although this is not to say that it is independent of the other BOTS. It is very much interlinked with the other three.
	Example of the ball as a reference point: The intensity with which you will defend when the ball is close to your goal is potentially different than when the ball is on the halfway line.
The following three BOTS are in no particular order of importance. Indeed, how these reference points interlink is the most important aspect of player decision-making.	

BOTS	Example
Opponent(s)	The position and numbers (plus strengths and weaknesses) of your opponent players will heavily influence what you do in the game, whether in or out of possession. Even the potential of what an opponent *might* do will affect your on-field decision-making. **Example of the opponent(s) as a reference point:** The concentrated positioning of the opponent's defensive block may lead players to play either *through*, *around*, or *over* them.
Team Mate(s)	In much the same way that your opponent will occupy spaces, have strengths and weaknesses, and have a predictable/unpredictable set of behaviours, so too will your teammates. These factors will, of course, affect all the decisions that players will make. **Example of the teammates (s) as a reference point:** A striker with the ball at a tight angle to goal may pass it to a teammate who is in a better position where it is easier to score (xG is higher).
Space	Space is essentially all the physical dimensions on a football field, covering everything from the physical make-up of the field of play – how close you are to sidelines/touchlines, whether you are in the penalty box, etc. – and also where the goals are relative to the other BOTS. You then have 'dynamic' spaces – these are not fixed spaces, but temporary gaps or 'pockets of space' that will pop up 'between the lines', 'in-behind' a defensive line, etc. **Example of space as a reference point:** A midfielder may pass the ball forward quicker if there is space behind the opponent's defensive line to exploit.

The examples above are intentionally basic to drive home the BOTS concept. Now that we understand BOTS, I am going to take things an extra step forward and create BOTS**S**.

State of the Game

Also impacting the decision of players is the *State of the Game* (or *Game State*). This is the story that the game is wrapped up in. It is where 'what-if' thinking comes from – what if we concede early, what if we have a player sent off, what if the opponent plays formation X when we expected formation Y, etc.? Game Sense is not exactly like other BOTS, but it further informs decision-making (if you are losing a cup final in the dying minutes, you would probably make riskier decisions than normal). Game State will include things like:

- The scoreline (the decision a player makes whilst leading 1-0 *may* be different than when losing 1-0)

- Big scorelines, for or against (if you are losing 4-0, you may play like you have nothing to lose; or winning 4-0, you may take more risks than usual)

- Momentum (if we are losing 3-0 but score the next goal, the momentum of the game can change wildly in our favour)

- The time of the match and the score at that time (the decision you make in the first minute *may* be different than the last)

- The opponent's formation (they play a GK:3-5-2, so we will try to attack early down the sides of their back 3)

- Wider implications like league position and game week (maybe you only need a draw to win a league, so with the score at 1-1, you may choose against chasing the win)

This list is not exhaustive. Literally, any game circumstance that affects the ebb-and-flow of the game can affect technical-tactical decision-making.

So, with so much change in football, how do coaches figure out tactics at all?

TACTICAL TASK 4

OUTLINE WHAT YOU WOULD DO WITH YOUR TEAM, BASED ON THE 'WHAT IF' SCENARIOS BELOW:

- Your team is blitzed early by the opposition and is 3-0 down after 15 minutes.

- You are leading 3-0 with 30 minutes to go.

- The score is 1-1 after 75 minutes. You need to hold on to secure a draw.

- You are leading 3-0 with 30 minutes to go.

- The score is 1-1 after 75 minutes, and you need to win.

- You need to win the last game of the season to win the league. The team you are playing is in first place and is two points ahead of you. Only a win will do.

- You are losing 2-0 with 10 minutes to go and have been chasing goals – you have just scored to make it 2-1. What is your approach for the final 10 minutes?

- Develop your own 'what-if' scenarios and solve them (maybe scenarios that have happened to you recently or historically).

Baseline Tactics

When discussing tactics, we do so – most of the time – when the perceived score is 0-0 and early in the game. Discussions on coaching courses, for example, rarely add State-of-the-Game 'what-ifs'. Indeed, many believe that it is these early 0-0 moments when a coach's true tactics are reflected by their team most – during the period when both teams are fresh, evenly matched, without momentum swings, and the result is not yet at stake. This is the period where you will most likely see the coach's main ideas.

Once past this stage, the game state takes on more and more significance.

Consider a game in which the team you coach (or a team that you watched live or on TV) was in the ebb-and-flow of a reasonably even, competitive game. Note how the behaviours change due to how the scoreline changes (and also other momentum-changing events (sendings-off, big chances, big chances missed, etc.)). As backed up by data, even at the highest levels of the game, teams who get into winning positions concede more and more possession to their opponent.

Consider your team is 2-0 down. How would you/your team react? I assume this would be different if this was the score at 18 minutes than it would be after 80 minutes? At 18 minutes, you may consider what the team needs to do to get a foothold in the game: stem the possibility of conceding further before building on this to score your way back into the game. At minute 80, this behaviour will be different. You would take more risks to score, probably accepting that in the chase to score goals, you may be weaker defensively and, therefore, have a higher potential to concede a third, but this may be considered an acceptable risk. Maybe the opponent will also be less concerned about scoring a third, allowing for more risk.

So, whilst the 0-0 sterile environment may be the first place we go when developing tactical ideas, studying potential 'what-if' moments are important too.

Your Style

How a coach and the players behave when important state-of-the-game moments arise can be telling and often different from coach to coach.

There is an insightful interview that Australian coach Ange Postecoglou gave to Rio Ferdinand and *TNT Sports* in 2023 (available on YouTube). Using video of his team, 'Ange' noted that, whilst winning 1-0 in the 44th minute of a game early in his tenure, the team's press stopped, and players were instead retreating to defend the lead and play down the clock until half-time. Whilst this would have been a strong strategy under their previous coach, Antonio Conte, it was no longer acceptable under the Greek/Australian.[5] In his eyes, if you call yourself a pressing team, then pressing and 'front-foot defending' was a *non-negotiable*, regardless of the game state.

TACTICAL TASK 5

WHAT ARE *YOUR* TACTICAL NON-NEGOTIABLES?

You may also remember, a very short time later, in a game against their bitter rivals Chelsea, when Tottenham were reduced to nine players. Instead of dropping back to protect the goal and run down the clock, Tottenham continued to hold a high defensive line – to the astonishment of virtually everyone else watching.

In Postecoglou's eyes, his team simply *had to* keep defending on the front foot. This was their *identity* as a pressing team or probably – more accurately – his identity as a pressing coach. He insisted that they carried on 'front-foot defending', even when conventional football wisdom thought he was crazy.

Ultimately, Tottenham lost the game, although they did create some moments when there was brief hope of getting something from the game. Postecoglou's stance, however, was about *more than one game* – more than winning a point or

---

[5] Interestingly, data provided by Ian Graham in his book *How to Win the Premier League* and *xGenius* by James Tippet (and many other data-driven football research) suggests that pushing on to try and score a second goal when leading 1-0 is a better bet for winning than sitting back and defending a lead.

losing all three.[6] Postecoglou wanted to leave his team in no doubt as to the habits and style he was expecting in the long term. *Nothing*, especially nothing so short-term as one half of one game was going to compromise this style. Jon MacKenzie summed it up perfectly in a *Tifo* video for *The Athletic* – "Why did Tottenham defend with a high line with nine men? For the same reason they defend with a high line with eleven men."

Whether you agree with Postecoglou or whether your attitude is more closely aligned with that of Conte is entirely up to you. Every coach will have their biases in certain situations, but *excellent coaches will not just dismiss one method over another without the full information*. Sure, holding a high defensive line with nine players versus 11 is probably not going to get you a result *today*, but the conviction of Postecoglou to his style was worth more to him than parking the bus to defend (and probably losing anyway!). As the saying goes – it is easier to be 100% committed to something than to be 98% committed (attributed to various people).

TACTICAL TASK 6

WHAT ARE *YOUR* COACHING BIASES?

---

[6] Interestingly, Tottenham played nine-man Liverpool around the same time. Whilst defending with nine players, Liverpool did not press, defended the box, but ultimately lost anyway.

Football Formations

TACTICAL TASK 7

I hear a lot of coaches say, "I don't like playing X formation".

DISCUSS WHY NOT. LIST THE MERITS OF THIS FORMATION. WHAT WOULD YOU DO IF YOU WERE FORCED TO PLAY THIS FORMATION?

(e.g., it is part of an Academy curriculum.)

Later in this book, we will again talk about Marcelo Bielsa – a coach with a very specific, methodical way of working, but also one who has inspired coaches the world over, despite the fact that he is far from the most "winningest" in the game.

The Argentine tactician is a very deep thinker about football and has proposed ten formations, as below (some variants of the same thing are often presented in other books, articles, or media – for example, a GK:4-3-1-2 is called a GK:4-4-2 'Diamond' in other areas). Getting a sample of Bielsa's thoughts is obviously beneficial but can also leave us with incomplete ideas. When I drew the formations below, I was sure that the Argentine may well see a different spread of players.

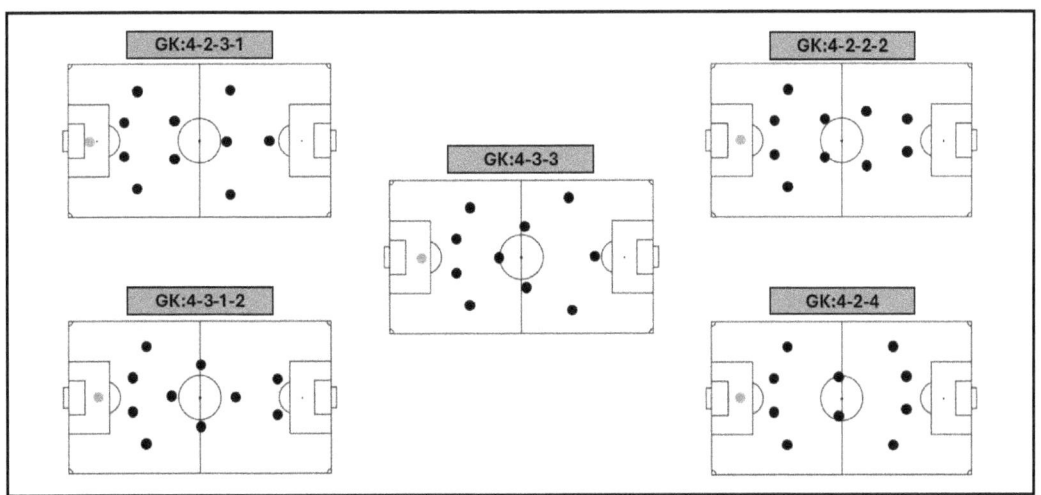

Bielsa's five Back-4 Formations

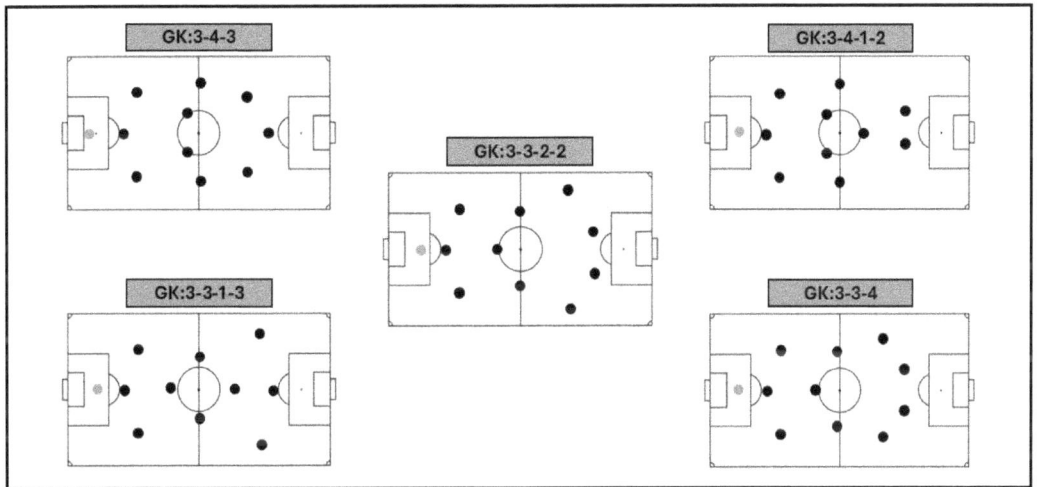

Bielsa's five Back-3 Formations

Formations have dominated tactical analysis since coaches first started to consider the spread of players around the field of play.

> # TACTICAL TASK 8
>
>
>
> When preparing for competition, and adding variety to our game, but also adding tactical development for players, I ask my coaches to have two 'go-to' formations (this can be more) – one with a Back 4 and one with a Back 3.
>
> **WHICH 4-AT-THE-BACK FORMATION(S) WOULD YOU PREFER WITH YOUR TEAM?**
>
> **WHICH 3-AT-THE-BACK FORMATION(S) WOULD YOU PREFER WITH YOUR TEAM?**
>
> (e.g., it is part of an Academy curriculum.)

I have historically said that formations are merely a starting point when we discuss tactics. What has been slow to evolve in coaching circles is the idea that the formation that we attribute to any team is rarely actually seen. For example, if you flew a drone over Manchester City's GK:4-3-3, you would very, very rarely see irrefutable evidence of four defenders, three midfielders and three forwards! You would probably struggle to present this drone evidence to someone who has never watched football and convince them of its GK:4-3-3-ness at all!

As it happens, Manchester City are as good an example as any to reinforce the point that formations start the conversation, and then everything just gets fluid, variable and dynamic. Once the ball rolls, they often begin their build-up with a back three, for example, and by the time it is in the opponent's defending third, the 'formation is probably GK:3-2-5 (potentially even GK:0-3-2-5 as their last defender is often midway through the opponent's half too!).

Others will say that you only really 'see' a formation when the team is out of possession (i.e., defending), but that idea is also pretty shallow. A team that plays GK:4-3-3 could easily be considered a GK:4-1-4-1, or a GK:3-4-3 could be called a GK:5-4-1 when in a low block.

If, then, we are going to show our players a visual, numerical representation of our formation, maybe we need to do so in a different way.

Your Base Formation

I like to rename what we traditionally call a 'formation' as a 'base formation'. It still uses numbered formations, like any of the ten that Bielsa suggests above, but we use it as the start of our conversation *instead of the end*. It is the centre upon which all variants revolve to give you and your players a starting point in how the team intends to move around the field dynamically. Shape-shifting, essentially.

The example below is not completely fictitious, but I had several teams rather than just one team in mind when I concocted it. It shows how a team can make slight positional alterations to a GK:4-3-3 that technically alters the formation, but only in specific phases of the game (a *re-formation*, if you like).

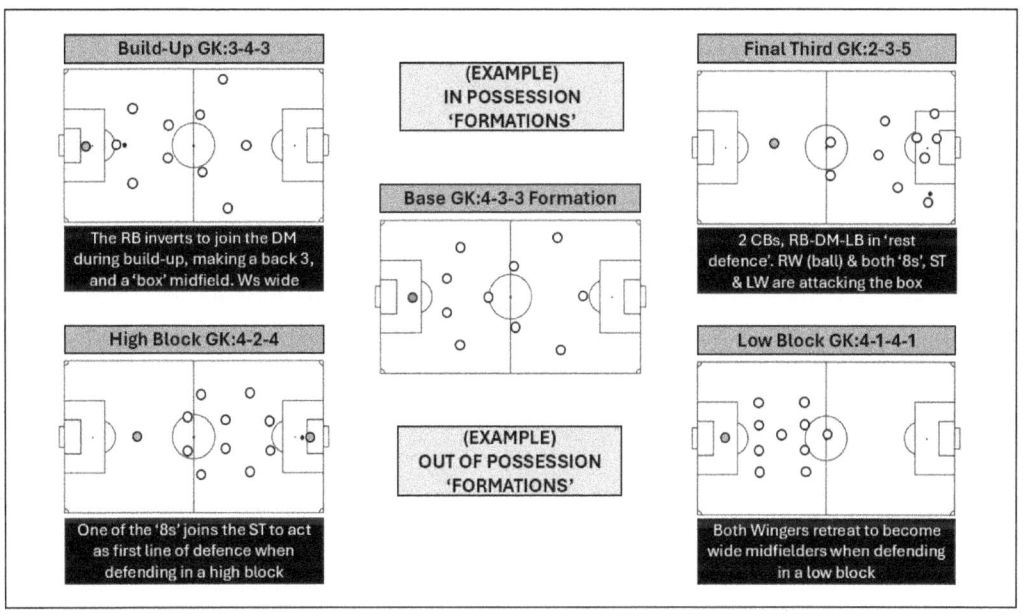

How a GK:4-3-3 base formation might morph during different phases of the game

Remember, as you read this (and read on through the book), that we are exploring examples of tactical work, *not complete truths*. Not every team that uses GK:4-3-3 as its base formation will build with an inverted full-back, and not all will defend high in a GK:4-2-4. These are examples dropped in throughout the book as potential 'lightbulb moments' for coaches, as you consider what that might look like in your team.

TACTICAL TASK 9

HOW MIGHT YOUR BASE FORMATION CHANGE IN DIFFERENT MOMENTS OF THE GAME?

This idea of changeable formations is not new. In Jed C. Davies' marvellous book, *The Philosophy of Football*, he notes how the terrific mid-1990s Ajax team would attack and defend in a different formation (as below).

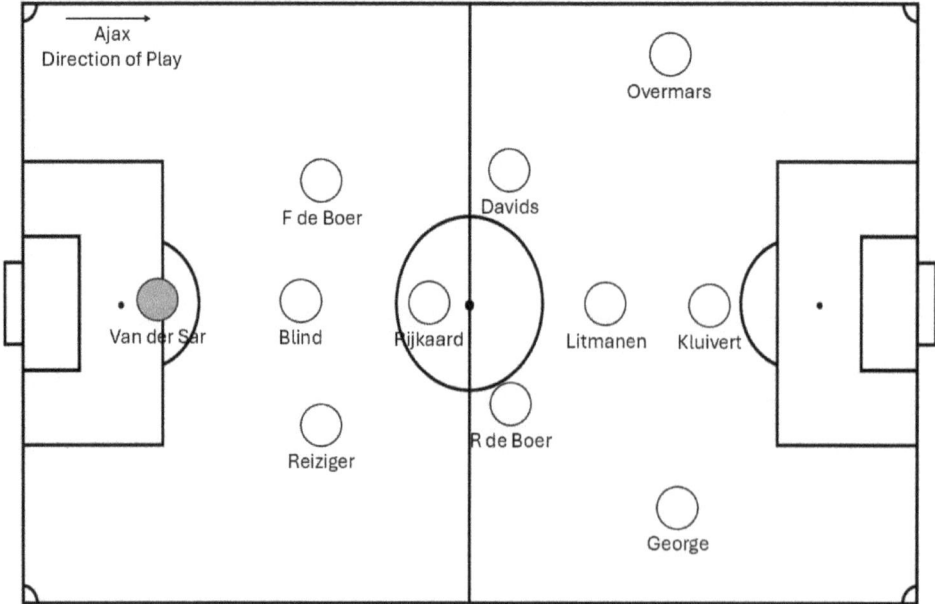

Ajax In Possession 3-3-1-3 Formation v AC Milan, Champions League Final, 1995

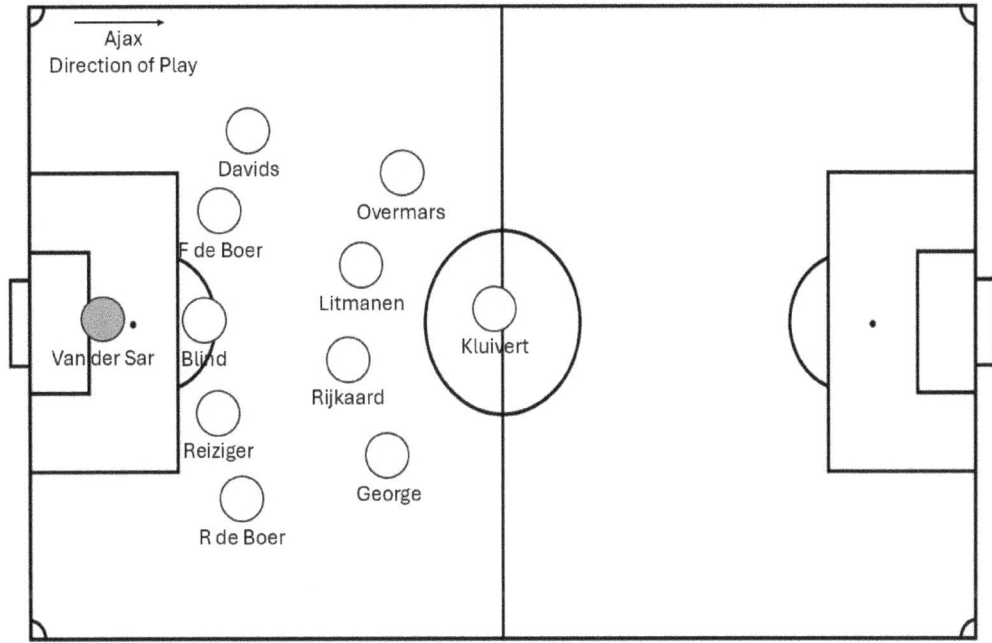

Ajax Out of Possession 5-4-1 Formation v AC Milan, Champions League Final, 1995

If this concept of fluid formations is new to you, you will start to see it everywhere, and will quite likely start to insist on it with your own team.

Players Change How Formations Function

A very strong, life-lasting lightbulb moment hit me as a young coach. I had moved clubs but coached the same age group at more-or-less the same level. I had my own blueprint, which included a way of playing that revolved around a GK:4-3-3 formation – and I used it with both teams.

I expected to lift the blueprint from one team to the next.

I expected my new team to play like my old one, but it didn't.

My 'play-off-two-touch', pass-it-sideways pivot midfielder changed to one who would take four or five touches and preferred to pass or drive forward. My box-to-box number 8 turned into one who hit one box with energy and enthusiasm but delayed returning to the box he had to defend! The left-footed wide-right attacker who dribbled inside to shoot was now a touchline pass-and-cross-it right midfielder (Think Salah v James Ward-Prowse). And so on… I had the same script but with different actors changing how the game looked and felt.

In 2022, John Muller of *The Athletic* published a thought-provoking article, *Introducing The Athletic's 18 Player Roles*. This article essentially data-fied my earlier lightbulb moment. It showed that by analysing the data and *habits* of players, you could (or maybe you *must*) move away from the traditional view of looking at a playing position (e.g., she is a right-back) and instead you look at a '"What *kind* of player have I got? What does this player like to do, and what are they tasked with doing?"

A summation of this study is below, with *The Athletic* defining 18 outfield types of players, as opposed to the six playing positions we have often referred to (although I did find it strange that there were no varieties of goalkeeper included).

Defence						Attack											
Wide Defender			Central Defender			Central Attacker			Wide Attacker			Advanced Midfielder			Deep Midfielder		
1. Overlapper	2. Progressor	3. Safety	4. Aggressor	5. Spreader	6. Anchor	7. Finisher	8. Target	9. Roamer	10. Wide Threat	11. Unlocker	12. Outlet	13. Box Crasher	14. Creator	15. Orchestrator	16. Box to Box	17. Distributor	18. Builder
James, Hakimi, Davies	Cancelo, Robertson, Alexander-Arnold	Wan-Bissaka, Castagne, Pavard	Araujo, Hernandez, Bastoni	Kounde, Militao, Marquinhos	Skriniar, De Ligt, Dias	Haaland, Martinez, Lukaku	Schick, Calvert-Lewin, Scamacca	Kane, Havertz, Richarlison	Mbappe, Vinicius, Salah	Mount, Neymar, Pellegrini	Sancho, Grealish, Felix	Foden, Wirtz, Gnabry	Fernandes, De Bruyne, Milinković-Savić	Bernardo, Bellingham, Barella	Camavinga, Ndidi, Fabinho	Tielemans, Fabian Ruiz, Kimmich	Tchouameni, Rodri, Rice

> **TACTICAL TASK 10**
>
>
>
> **LIST THE PLAYERS IN YOUR TEAM. THEN, LIST THEIR PLAYING POSITIONS(S), BEFORE FINALLY LISTING WHICH OF THE 18 'PLAYER ROLES' THEY MAY FIT.**

The concoction of different individuals that make up your team – with their different habits and traits – means that while we may model our team tactics on A, B, or C, the outcome you see on game day may look different.

So, whilst tactics help to predict what a game of football *might* look like, flexibility in thinking is always a prerequisite for any coach.

Conclusion

Your *Baseline Tactics* will be a culmination of much of what we discussed throughout this chapter:

The Four Moments of the Game

How this relates to *Your Playing Style*

Your *Formations* (plural is intentional) and how they may dynamically change during different moments of the game

The *individual make-up* of the players you have.

Completing the assigned tasks, in addition to the reading, will help strengthen any learning from the chapter and help you put ideas for your team all in one place!

Moving Forward Through Superiorities

Over the course of the rest of this book, we will use the above to explore football tactics further, and this time, through the use of superiorities – i.e., being better than the opponent in certain areas at certain times.

TACTICAL TASK 11 – LIGHTBULB MOMENT

Early in this chapter, I suggested that all coaches are tactically deficient in some area. At the end of each chapter, I will therefore set you the task below:

WHAT WAS YOUR GREATEST LIGHTBULB MOMENT FROM THIS CHAPTER?

I am not asking you to list a bunch of things – and the lightbulb moment could either be a deficiency or an idea you had reinforced – either way, I want you to use this lightbulb moment for improvement. Zoom in on the lightbulb moment – it will probably be the concept that has given you the most food for thought. Now, ask yourself...

HOW CAN I IMPROVE MY UNDERSTANDING OF THIS LIGHTBULB MOMENT?

Introducing Superiorities
(Simply!)

Arguably, the USP of my coaching books is the intentional simplicity involved. Sometimes, I click on a very enticing coaching article, only to find the ideas presented in a way that is next-to-impossible to understand with any clarity. I am a firm believer that it is necessary to make complex ideas easy for the reader and coach to understand – but then challenging (in a positive way) to implement. It is like the "support and challenge" mantras of many football coaches!

Superiorities

I find the topic of superiorities in football to be one of these ideas that has been made more complicated than it needs to be – and often makes members of the coaching fraternity look away, close the book, or shut down the article link in frustration. This is often due to what we could call the "paralysis of over-complication". Here, however, I am confident that you will not just gain an understanding of superiorities in football, but be able to apply them to your football team and football matches through the use of the tasks, but also through the inherent value of the concepts.

Five Superiorities

There are five types of superiorities in a game of football that we are going to indulge ourselves in over the upcoming chapters and tasks:

1. *Numerical Superiority* – We have more players than you.
2. *Qualitative Superiority* – We have better players than you.
3. *Positional Superiority* – We have players in better positions than yours.

4. *Cooperative Superiority* – Our players play better together than yours.
5. *Dynamic Superiority* – Our players move/adapt/make better decisions than yours.

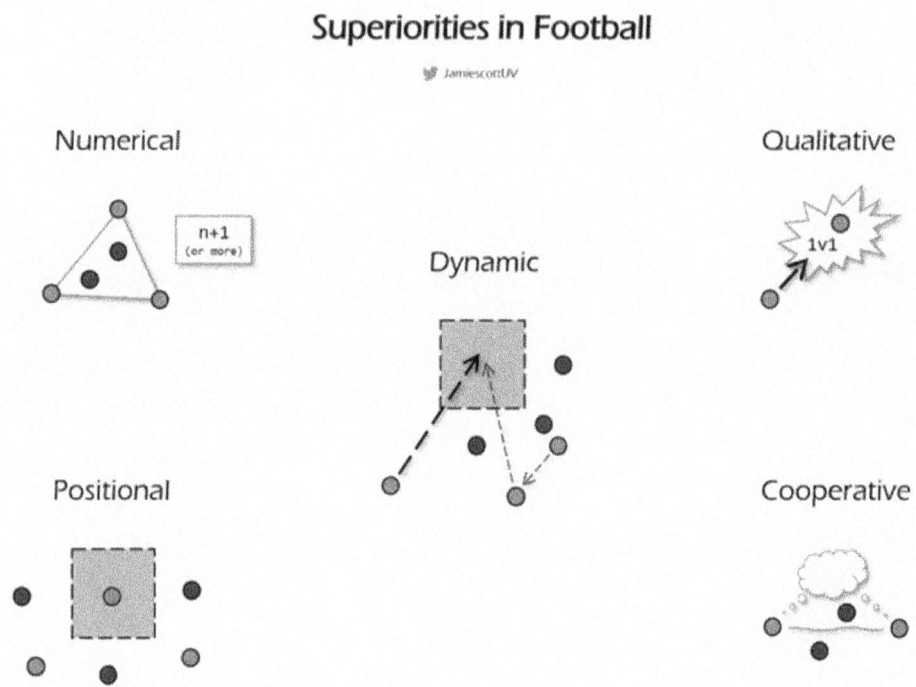

Football's Five Superiorities

TACTICAL TASK 12

WHAT DO YOU UNDERSTAND ABOUT EACH SUPERIORITY?

WHICH ONE DO YOU KNOW BEST AT THIS POINT?

Each of the following four chapters – which make up the 'meat' of the book – will be based on the following superiorities (with the tasks to reflect them):

1. Numerical
2. Qualitative
3. Positional
4. Cooperative

The fifth superiority – Dynamic – will be dealt with in all four chapters as we explore how this superiority, in particular, is completely *inseparable* from any of the others, and needs to be detailed within the contexts of the others.

You will notice that some sections and some tasks will require you to bring multiple superiorities together. They are, after all, just like the *Four Corners of Player Development* and The *Four Moments of the Game* that we spoke about in the Introduction chapter, five *interlinking components* of the game that we can study in isolation before fitting them back into the whole of the game.

The first superiority we will study together is the most basic – numerical superiority – and it is probably this one that all coaches deal with first.

TACTICAL TASK 13 – LIGHTBULB MOMENT

WHAT WAS YOUR GREATEST LIGHTBULB MOMENT FROM THIS CHAPTER?

HOW CAN YOU IMPROVE YOUR UNDERSTANDING OF THIS IDEA?

Numerical Superiority

We Have More Players Than You

One hundred years ago, if you attended a high-level football game, you would have seen a conscious understanding of numbers and the early efforts to organise 11 players into a shape that would offer enough *spread* around the pitch to attack and defend effectively (although the priority was to attack!). The opposing 11 players would attempt to do the same thing, and the tactical football match was born in its most basic form. This action and interaction between two XIs remains the essence of the tactical coaching of a game of football and its first question… how do we effectively cover the pitch with our players to score more goals than the opponent?

Over time, numbers have formed a huge part of football, and finding ways to achieve numerical superiority within the game is something we will explore heavily here. It is vital, though, that our superiorities journey does not end with *only* thinking about the numbers game.

Having more numbers or fewer numbers is quite easy to define. Whilst numbers are the best starting point in understanding superiorities in football, they come nowhere near completing the football tactical story, even though we often speak and think about them as such. There is, instead, a constant interaction between numerical superiority and the other superiorities involved in the game.

A Game of 1v0 – 11v11

I am a chess novice. When I play chess, I see the pawn and the move the pawn can make. I see the bishop and how it should move. I only see checkmate when checkmate is highly visible.

Elite chess players, however, see these individual things (of course) but they also see how they *interlink* with the other pieces, the opposition, and the wider game. They know, even as the game pieces become spread around the board, what the *overall, single structure* of that game looks like. They see the pawn or the bishop's role within the context, pattern, and shape of the game. They have an understanding of what the opposition 'coach' might do – his or her game tactics. In comparison, I just move a pawn or a castle and hope for the best until the next move!

The way I play chess is the equivalent of ball-watching in football. *Most* supporters, for example, do this exclusively. They watch one on-ball action, then the next one, then the next one, etc. As coaches, and as you *develop* as a coach, you learn to see the bigger picture and connect the pieces and individual events together. If you put 23 players on the pitch, for example, a novice would likely not notice (or would have to do a player count) to prove there are one-too-many players within the structure of the game. An experienced eye, however, would quickly 'feel' that something was different or structurally amiss. As *dynamic* as the game is, we can see patterns and how pieces could and should link together.

Within coach education circles, we have traditionally called these different ways of seeing the game as being focused in three ways:

1. On the ball
2. Around the ball
3. Away from the ball

FC Barcelona, through the *Barcelona Innovation Hub*, the academic department of the club, have a slightly different way of labelling this:

1. Zone 0 (individual skills)
2. Zone 1 (players who are in direct support of the player on the ball)
3. Zone 2 (cooperation – the wider tactical game)

Below is a visual of these three zones in action. The smallest circle is where the 'On the Ball' (barcelona's "Zone 0") action is, with the black centre-back in possession and being challenged by the white striker. Surrounding this action is the 'Around the Ball' area (Zone 1), occupied by the players who may have the most direct, imminent impact on the ball, supporting their teammates both in and out of possession. Finally, we see the largest 'Away from the Ball' (Zone 2) region, which involves all the players.

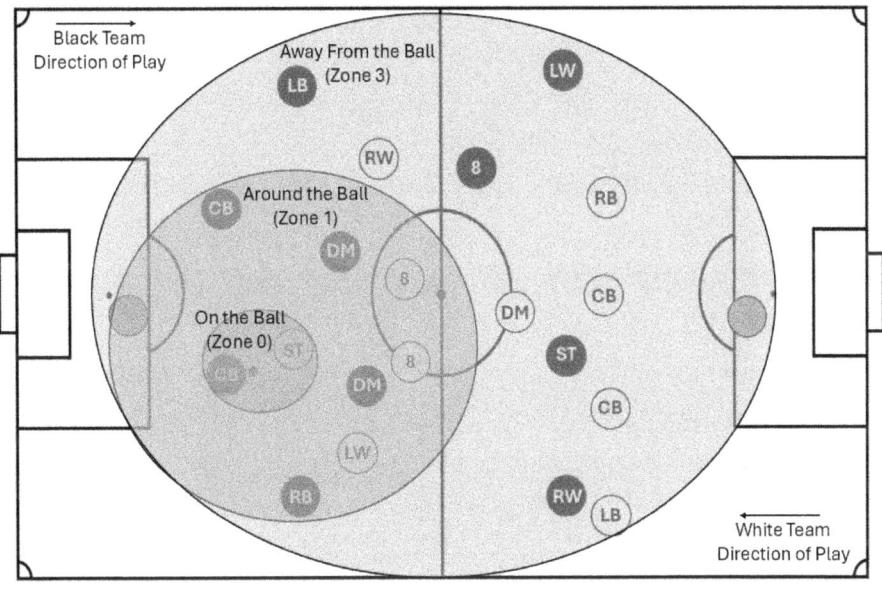

As mentioned, most fans (and novice coaches) will focus almost exclusively on the ball. This component is, of course, the most important reference point. What happens with the ball is ultimately what will decide the game. It is the 'present' – but, around this nucleus, the rest of the game is also happening. Players' movements and positioning (especially in relation to what the opposition is doing) will directly impact the game's near future (e.g., if a striker loses the ball *now*, our centre-back is way out of position and will lead to the potential concession of a big chance).

By fostering focus *around the ball* and *away from the ball*, you are not trying to avoid seeing what the ball is doing, but you are trying to access the game a few moves ahead, rather than amateurly jumping from now to now. Therefore, improving our view of the game is a crucial factor in truly understanding the game. If you keep playing chess one move at a time, you will invariably lose against those who have become better at anticipating and seeing the bigger game.

TACTICAL TASK 14

THE NEXT TIME YOU ARE COACHING (OR WATCHING) A MATCH (ENSURE YOU HAVE A VIEW OF THE FULL PITCH), MAKE A CONSCIOUS EFFORT TO:

- CONCENTRATE YOUR FOCUS: AROUND THE BALL*
- CONCENTRATE YOUR FOCUS: AWAY FROM THE BALL*

NOTE HOW IT FELT. PRACTISE AGAIN. DEVELOP THE HABIT OF SHIFTING FOCUS BETWEEN ALL THREE AREAS, AS NECESSARY. IF YOU NEED ANOTHER WAY TO THINK ABOUT IT:

FOCUS YOUR ATTENTION ON THE NEXT PHASE OF THE GAME (IF YOUR TEAM HAS THE BALL, FOCUS ON WHAT WILL HAPPEN WHEN YOU LOSE IT. IF YOU ARE DEFENDING, FOCUS YOUR ATTENTION ON WHAT COULD HAPPEN WHEN YOU REGAIN THE BALL).

* DON'T WORRY ABOUT MISSING SOMETHING ON THE BALL (YOU WILL STILL SEE MOST OF THIS AS YOU HAVE TO KNOW WHERE THE BALL IS TO FOCUS AWAY FROM IT!). THE BITS YOU MAY MISS WILL BE RELAYED TO YOU, AS EVERYONE ELSE WILL PROBABLY JUST BE FOLLOWING THE BALL. FEEL FREE TO DEPLOY YOUR ASSISTANT COACH AS

> **THE EXCLUSIVE ON-BALL WATCHER WHILE YOU DIVERT YOUR ATTENTION INTO THE NEAR FUTURE!**

In addition to the traditional and Barcelona method, above, we can also relabel and reframe this idea by carving the game up into smaller *numerical* segments:

- On the Ball – Zone 0 – A Game of 1v1 (1v0)
- Around the Ball – Zone 1 – A Game of Smaller Games
- Away from the Ball – Zone 2 – A Game of 11v11

A Game of 1v1s (1v07)

One of the earliest formations that became widely adopted in the game was known as the 'WM' – the letters reflecting the shape of the team, as below. At that point in time, nobody felt the need to put "1" or "GK" before the letters, as the goalkeeper's presence was – naturally – a given. The establishment of this formation is widely credited to the 1920s Arsenal coach, Herbert Chapman,[8] and quickly became the de facto formation across the highest levels of the game.

---

[7] 1v0 is just a condensed way of saying that a player will have the ball but will not be under pressure from an opponent *in that moment*. The goalkeeper in possession, or a set-play situation, may be the most obvious examples of this, although an outfield player in open play may often be unopposed in moments during open play, too.

[8] *You will notice the names of some playing positions that we still use today, although in slightly different contexts (the evolution of the game saw the addition of one of the 'centre-halves' to the backline, hence turning 'full-backs' into wide defenders, but all that is for another book!).*

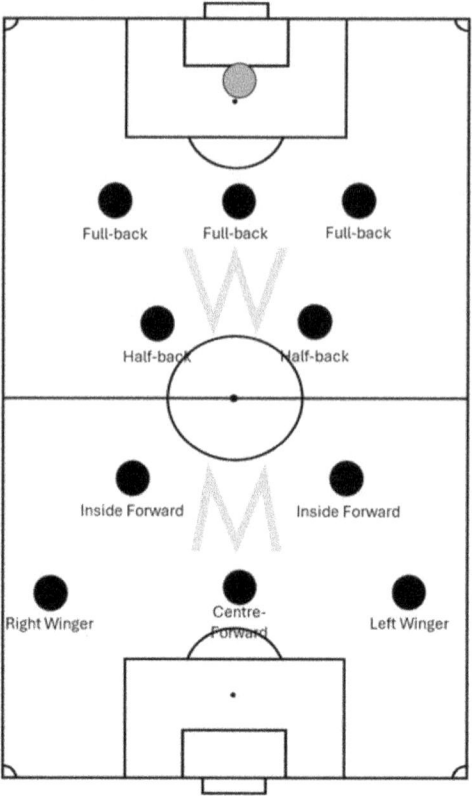

The 'WM' Formation

I am a firm believer, certainly at grassroots and amateur (and often at pro and semi-pro) levels, that we still overuse concepts that originated in the era of WM, especially the idea of 1v1s or "individual battles".

When WM played against WM, football was almost separated into a game of ten individual duels (plus goalkeepers, obviously) that took place all over the pitch (see below[9]). Winning your "individual battle" became the cornerstone of winning a game. If 6/10 outfield players could dominate their direct opponents most of the time, then, by this logic, the team should dominate and win the game.

---

[9] In practice, it often also led to two separate 5v5 attack v defence games either side of the halfway line.

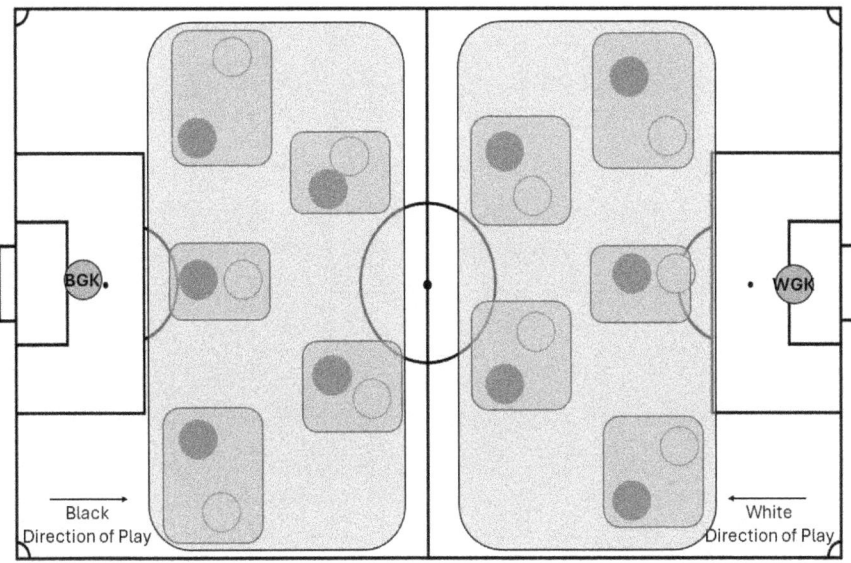

The WM Formations of both teams meant that games became a sequence of 1v1 'battles'.

Even up until the popularisation of the GK:4-4-2 formation in the 1980s, 90s, and early 2000s, this view of the game as a battlefield of 1v1 duels remained evident – centre-backs v strikers, midfielder v midfielder, winger v full-back, etc. Away from the top level, this concept is still alive today and is probably one of the biggest parts of the tactical game that needs updating.

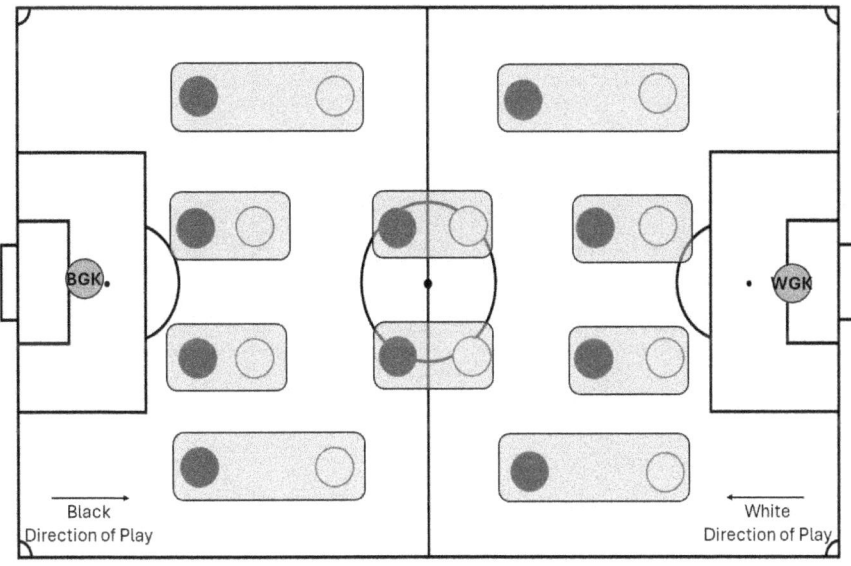

GK:4-4-2 v GK:4-4-2 as a game of 1v1s

While I have no issues with 1v1s and duels, we witness a game nowadays that is much more complex and dynamic than that reductionist view. It is not that 1v1 duels no longer exist – there are plenty throughout a game – it is a recognition that they no longer exist in isolation.

A winger and full-back may have numerous duels throughout a game, but these are rarely exclusive battles for 90+ minutes. Wingers not only swap wings frequently, but they also play inside a lot more, for example. Full-backs now also play inside.

You most commonly see games where two defenders versus one striker is the norm. Indeed, many central defender pairings now struggle to defend 2v2, something that was once considered their most important attribute.[10] Support players are soon added if a player is struggling 1v1, whether in attack or defence (e.g., an overlapping full-back helps support his winger in a 1v1 attacking duel, or indeed a winger drops back to create a 2v1 in defensive situations). In a wonderful webinar that The Athletic's Jon MacKensie did on Hybrid Defending, he noted that in a certain moment versus Manchester City, Arsenal winger Gabriel Martinelli was given the responsibility for either applying pressure to the opponent's full-back (his direct 1v1), or their central midfield player or their advanced playmaker, Kevin de Bruyne. His eventual on the ball action (i.e., who he defends), of course, depended on what happened with the ball.

---

[10] Football logic may therefore suggest that if the modern centre-back pairing cannot cope with two strikers, then we may soon see the *widespread* re-popularisation of the two-striker partnership. Which may, in turn, see an increase in three-centre-back formations. In other words, both teams searching for numerical advantages.

> **TACTICAL TASK 15**
>
>
>
> **CONSIDER HOW YOU CAN COMMUNICATE THE IDEA OF EACH POSITION HAVING 'HYBRID' DUTIES TO YOUR PLAYERS.**
>
> **FOR EXAMPLE, I ONCE WORKED WITH A COACH WHO WOULD TELL PLAYERS THAT THEY HAD "A-JOB-AND-A-HALF" – THE DUTIES OF THEIR OWN POSITION, PLUS A CONTRIBUTION TO THE DUTIES OF THOSE AROUND THEM (THE 'HALF' WAS NOT INTENDED TO BE TAKEN LITERALLY).**

As a result, the idea (and the saying) that my direct opponent is "my man" or "her marker" is now a real bugbear in some coaching circles. A player can no longer legitimately defer responsibility for poor defending if the opposing player "wasn't 'my man'" and if they were the player most suitable to defend the danger at that moment. Indeed, high-level managers will bemoan players who are unwilling to share defensive responsibility for multiple players in moments. A teammate may be defending 1v1 in the penalty box, for example, but she shouldn't need to do so for any longer than necessary, before backup support or cover arises.

Players and coaches who see the game exclusively through this traditional 1v1 prism are missing a trick and are failing to acknowledge that the game is a lot more dynamic than that. Remnants of this thinking may well be the reason why many novice coaches tend to just follow the ball. Sure, the ball is the centrepiece – the main 'BOT' – but we need to be comfortable chunking bigger parts of the game together.

A Game of Smaller Games?

Whilst we acknowledge that football as an aggregation of ten 1v1 duels is far too simplistic (whilst conceding that 1v1 duels are still very prominent), we can form an understanding of the game by breaking it down into its *around the ball* segments – and this method is used by a lot more coaches than you may realise, even in the professional game.

The pitch below, for example, is an adaptation from numerous pieces of work from Michael Beale. Beale is popularly known in the professional game for managing QPR, Rangers, and Sunderland, and for his work as assistant coach to Steven Gerrard. He is less well-known, perhaps, in his capacity working for the Academies at Chelsea and Liverpool, for his social media presence, or how much coaching literature he has published.

Inherent in Beale's approach to the game is to treat the full 11v11 as a set of smaller games that range from 1v1 to 3v3. As an Academy coach, he would base his Foundation Phase (players up to 11/12 years old) sessions on players being able to master playing these 'small-sided games'. As a coach of adult professionals, he continues to use these games as tactical preparation for the many "mini-games" that arise during the course of a match.

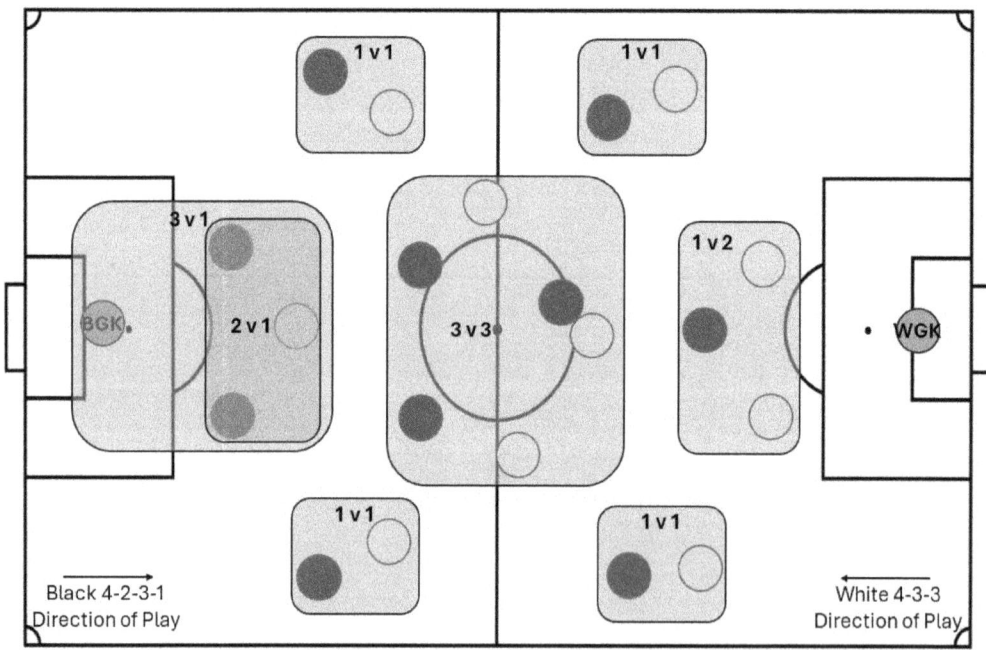

Michael Beale's view of the game as a series of interconnected small-sided games

> **TACTICAL TASK 16**
>
>
>
> **CONSIDER YOUR TEAM AND YOUR FORMATION. WHAT AREAS OF THE PITCH WILL YOUR TEAM HAVE THE MOST NATURAL NUMERICAL SUPERIORITIES? HOW CAN YOU CHANGE YOUR TEAM OR FORMATION TO GENERATE MORE OF THESE ADVANTAGES? IF YOU INCREASE NUMERICAL SUPERIORITY IN ONE AREA, WHERE ARE YOU LOSING IT? ARE YOU HAPPY TO TRADE THIS OFF?**

The Game as 11v11

Marcelo Bielsa is notorious for his obsessive and methodological approach to setting up his football teams. He is also, arguably, well known as one of the most extreme coaches when it comes to breaking the game down into its smallest parts in training sessions – similar in concept, if not in execution, to Beale above.

The key, however, to breaking the game down into smaller parts, is how they *fit back together* – how the 'micro' pieces fit into the 'macro' structure. How *all* of the pieces on a chess board move and interact together, both white and black, and give rise to the game we see to its fullest. One method Bielsa uses for this is to be *reactive*[11] (numerically, not stylistically) to the formation and set-up of the opposition.

---

[11] Some coaches you can either categorise as 'proactive' or 'reactive' to the opposition. Bielsa is reactive in this situation, but proactive in terms of his team's playing *style*. As verified by a member of his staff, *El Loco* will adapt his formation then put his aggressive, energetic, man-marking style "on top" of this formation.

When an opponent sets up in Formation X, Bielsa will use a formation that:

1. Has numerical superiority in his back line – i.e., he will have one more defender than the opponent will have attackers (+1)
2. Has numerical equality in his midfield line (=); and
3. This, therefore, leaves him with numerical inferiority in his front line (-1)

Below, I have included two examples of this approach:

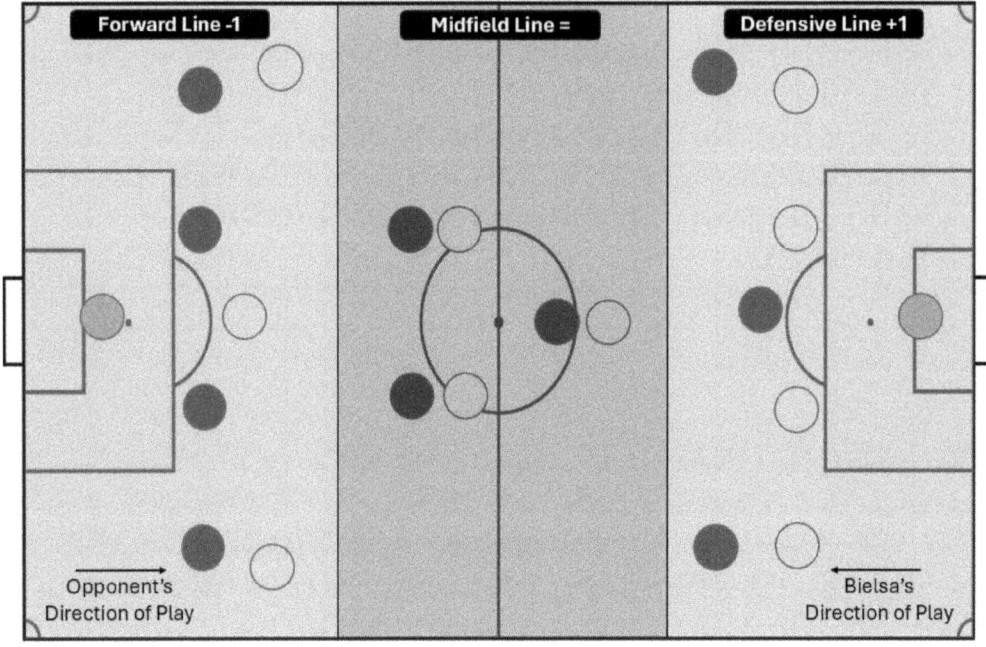

Bielsa's numerical approach when playing against a GK:4-2-3-1 formation

TACTICAL TASK 17

USING BIELSA'S (+1) (=) (-1) APPROACH, SET UP A TEAM TO FACE THE FORMATIONS BELOW.

You v GK:3-4-3 Formation

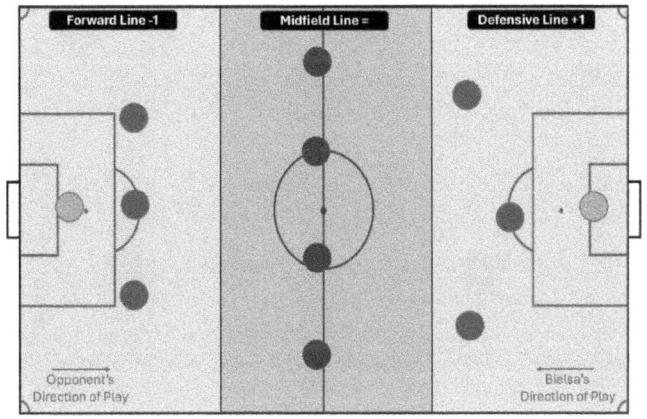

You v GK:4-1-2-1-2 (GK:4-4-2 'Diamond' Midfield)

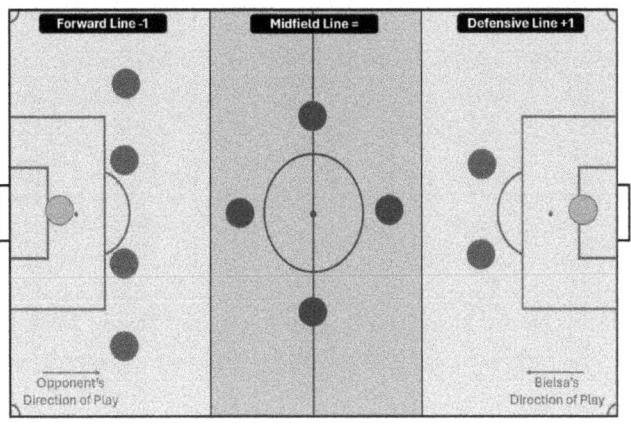

Whilst the game itself is 11v11 and even-numbered (for the most part) as a whole, we can – as Bielsa does – play with our positioning of players to create *overloads* in certain areas of the pitch. So, for example, as you can below, you have two centre-backs against one striker, or a four-player box of two number 6's and two number 10's playing against a three-man midfield.

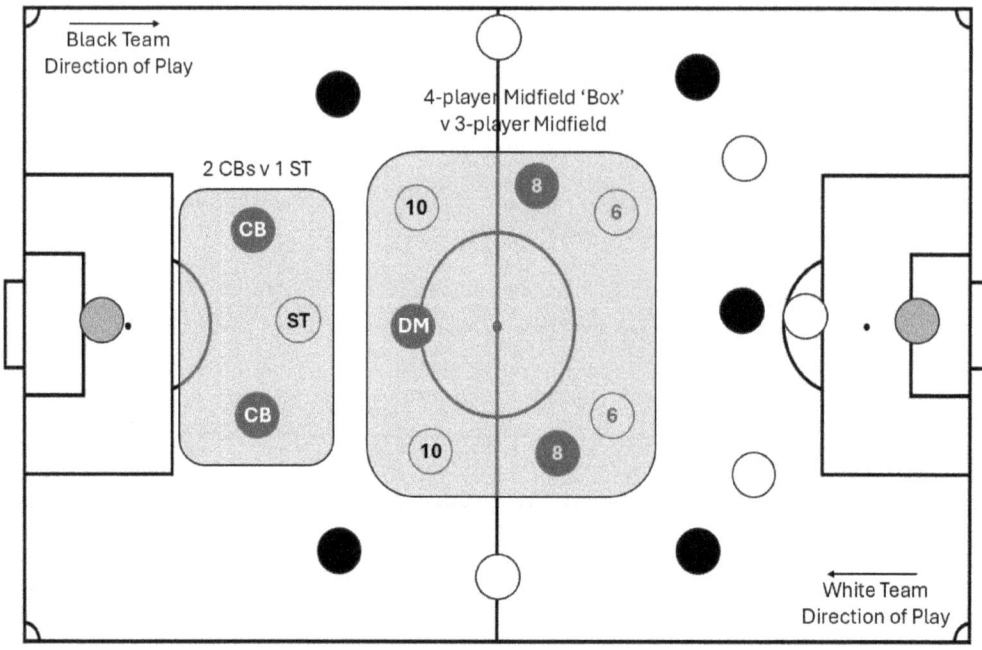

Examples of natural overloads within the structure of an 11v11 game

Each 11v11 game you see will have this numerical battle between opposing formations. Some formations lend themselves to having natural advantages or disadvantages in certain areas, as above. Regardless of what formations you or your opponent choose, both of you will likely have a natural structural numerical superiority around certain pitch areas.

You could call this idea *static numerical superiority*. In other words, should players remain in this structure, they would retain whatever numerical advantages or disadvantages they may have on paper.

However, football is not a static game, and formations are not static either, despite what is often visualised to us pre-game on a TV matchday broadcast. Formations are, in fact, alive.

TACTICAL TASK 18

DRAW YOUR FORMATION. PIT IT AGAINST THE MAIN FORMATIONS YOU PLAY AGAINST. WHERE ARE YOUR NATURAL NUMERICAL ADVANTAGES AND DISADVANTAGES?

Dynamic Numerical Superiority

Our next and most crucial step in understanding numerical superiority is moving from our static ideas of the game and formations to the dynamic. We must delve beyond the natural numerical superiorities that the interactions of different formations produce, so we can see the game and the positioning of players in a much more fluid way… it's the true game that exists away from the tactics board. The fluid nature of player positioning is a key concept in understanding the tactical game.

You will notice that so far in this book, I have used the word *moment* in *italics* quite frequently. This is completely intentional to emphasise just how dynamic a game of football is, and how it should be seen. A static formation stays forever on a tactics board – real football sees a dynamic process where there are patterns and principles and game-changing events that often last only for a moment. The moment a player appears 'between the lines', before the passing lane to them is shut down by the opponent. The moment a weak-side full-back does not cover the back-post area and the winger ghosts past her. The moment you outnumber the opponent, before quickly losing that advantage as the opposition reacts.

Football is a *variable game*. In other words, things change quickly and regularly. There is no restriction on player movement – a left full-back can pop up at right-wing; a striker can head the ball away from under his own crossbar; even a goalkeeper can move freely around the field. Whilst we use formations and numbers to organise the spread of players, there is still a freedom of movement. Players can even take up offside positions and not break the rules because of when or how they get involved in the play again.

As modern coaches, however, we must free ourselves from the reliance on over-prescribing and thinking of the game in a static rather than a fluid, dynamic capacity. One example I often hear is of coaches endorsing the "stick to your position" mantra with players. Whilst not definitively incorrect, blanket ideas like this throw limits over players rather than encourage an exploration of the limits of any given position. This, in turn, reduces this wonderful game to a robotic entity – often just so unimaginative coaches can make sense of it. Imagine instead the problems you could cause opposition teams by prescribing a fluid version of playing positions and football tactics!

Out of Possession Dynamic Numerical Superiority

(Having more defenders than they have attackers!)

Opposition's Half[12]

Teams pressing in the final third are usually -1 or even -2 if you include the opponent's goalkeeper. Teams will normally task their main presser(s) to use their 'cover-shadow' to cut off passes and 'make play predictable' to reduce this deficit – to try and temporarily create equality of numbers. These pressing teams may often use 'traps' to send opponents into congested areas to regain the ball.

We must note, however, that there are teams that are quite happy to defend with *even numbers* when the ball is in the final third, and actively seek out a way of defending player-to-player (usually with the goalkeeper still free)[13],

---

[12] In this section, I will use 'halves' and 'thirds' to donate areas of the field – this is for simplicity only. In a dynamic football match, these zones are philosophical and not just physical areas. For example, you will often see teams still in a build-up phase while deep in their opponent's half, or a defender carrying out 'emergency defending' on the halfway line to stop a goal-scoring opportunity. These lines often blur.

[13] The GK being the free player is an interesting concept, used much more by coaches in recent years. The GK is the most likely to be the free player in a man-to-man press, although their movements are still more restricted by positional boundaries than that of an outfield player.

especially when high pressing the ball. Italian Serie A side Atalanta famously and comprehensively beat German side Bayer Levekusen 3-0 in the UEFA Europa League Final in 2024, using this very tactic. As the German side built from the back, the Serie A opponent slipped out of their zonal structure and pressed hard, high, and with equal numbers to disrupt this build-up, which was the trademark of Leverkusen's exceptional 2023-24 season (this was the only defeat they had suffered). The drawback for many is that player-to-player in the final third will mean player-to-player in their defensive third, too, opening up the risk of high balls or opposition attacks if this initial press is beaten.

Our Half

Once high defending turns into defending in your half, however, even teams like Atalanta will dynamically revert to overloading the attacking team.

It is hardly a revolutionary idea that most coaches seek numerical superiority when defending in their own half, or certainly as we start to defend our own defensive third, penalty box, and the goal itself. Like Bielsa, once organised defensively, most coaches and teams will have more defenders than attackers. There may, of course, be *situational* moments where attackers will outnumber defenders due to the dynamic interactions of both teams. These are usually counter-attacks or very, very brief random moments or defensive errors. Such is the unusual nature of attackers outnumbering defenders, we sometimes hear very excited commentators exclaim how it's "four versus two" or "they have a player-over at the back post" etc.

In Possession Dynamic Numerical Superiority

(Having more attackers than they have defenders!)

First Third ('Build-Up')

Barcelona's La Masia Academy consistently speaks about creating overloads and 'free players' in their own half – and the diagram below is taken from the wonderful *Barcelona Innovation Hub* material around these build-up concepts.

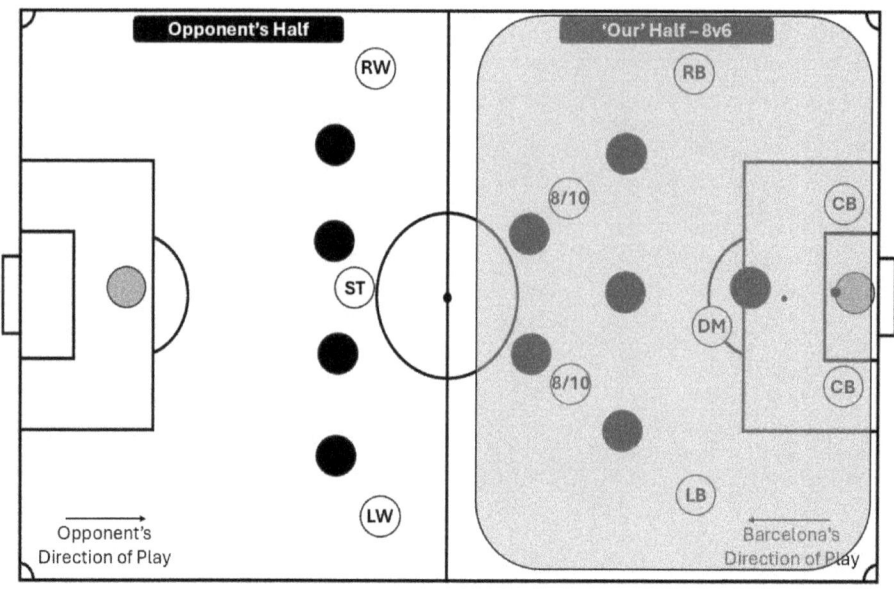

Barcelona creating numerical superiority in their own first third

The above diagram shows a snapshot of what the BIH teaches us about positioning at goal kicks. Simply put, the three strikers start by pinning four defenders in their half (defenders playing with a +1). By doing so, Barcelona can play 8v6 in their own half. Even if one of the opponent's backline gets involved in the press and makes it an 8v7 later down the line, there is still a free player (most often the goalkeeper). Having one free player is an essential aspect of positional play, but there is a significant difference and value in who is most valuable for this. Having your goalkeeper as the free player will help the team retain and recycle possession, for example. But if your number 10 is the free player, you can suddenly break the press, advance, and progress up the field.

Middle Third ('Progress & Penetrate the Ball')

When in possession, the middle third (remember, the philosophical middle third, not necessarily the physical, geographical middle third of the field) is usually the main battle for any kind of superiority, with the central idea being that if you can dominate midfield, you can dominate games. This often first translates to dominating with numbers, so much so that modern teams can use any of the following dynamic movements to have players 'arrive' in central midfield zones, all of which were considered quite radical not so long ago:

- Full-backs inverting (e.g., Trent Alexander-Arnold)
- Centre-backs stepping into midfield positions (e.g., John Stones)
- Wingers inverting to central positions (e.g., virtually all of them now!)
- Central midfield players starting in wide positions (e.g., Jude Bellingham)
- False 9s (e.g., Lionel Messi)

This seemingly 'all-roads-lead-to-midfield' attitude of a whole generation of coaches and players is grounded in gaining numerical superiority in midfield, but is based on players *arriving into these positions* rather than starting or even waiting in those spaces, a very important concept.

Final Third ('Create & Score')

Often, in the final third, the opponent will insist on outnumbering you, so being 'just' numerically *equal* is actually a highly sought-after advantage. Being 1v1 against a full-back or 2v2 against a pair of centre-backs, even just for a moment, is considered of high value to the attacking team. Teams may often try to 'overload to isolate' defenders in numerically equal situations. Here, a team will intentionally overload one side of the field to draw opposition numbers to the ball, before switching play to isolate the opposite full-back in a 1v1 situation against a winger.

Chelsea coach Enzo Maresca (like many others), however, goes one step further and speaks openly about trying to create dynamic situations where the opponent's back four will have to defend against five attackers, for example. The diagram below shows how this 5v4 may also produce some other smaller +1 advantages in certain moments. Other numerical superiority ideas in the final third will include an attempt to isolate a full-back 2v1, for example.

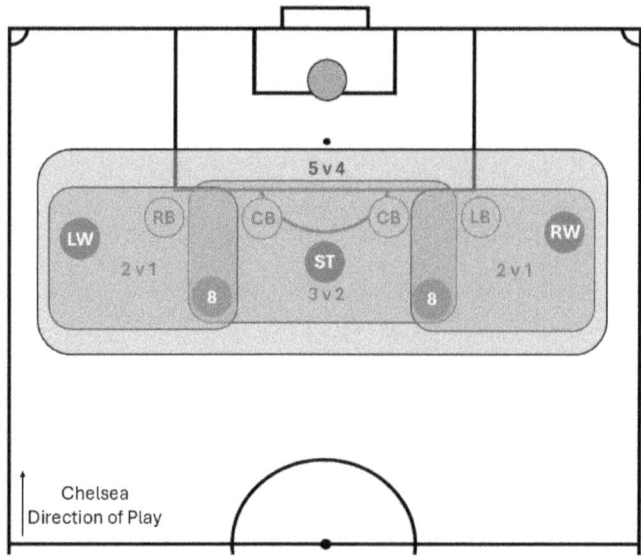

Maresca's Chelsea searching for overloads in the final third

Transitional Dynamic Numerical Superiority

(Having more defenders when we lose the ball / Having more players (equal players?) available to attack when we win the ball)

Transition to Defend (Losing the Ball)

Rest defence is a term used when a team is attacking to ensure they are 'secure' in defence, which usually involves being 'numbers up'. For example, while you attack, the opposing team leaves one striker up-field, and you deploy two defenders (+1) to counter that. If they leave two, you may leave three, and so on.[14] It is essentially a tactic that prepares for the moment when you lose possession of the ball; it is designed to prevent you from being counter-attacked and your goal threatened too easily.

Remember, the dynamic part of the game means that this is not a rule but, rather, common practice. Many teams will go 1v1 in these moments, too. Some teams, in some moments, may even rest-defend with "+2" (which makes pressing difficult as the opponent will be +2 closer to where the ball

---

[14] You might find teams, players, and coaches engage in a 'cat-and-mouse' game with this. Who is braver to accept equal numbers or underloads in what area?!

is). Brentford FC, the English club whose on-field decisions are guided by deep statistical analysis, have even been known to attack corners with all ten outfield players in and around the opponent's penalty area. Data-based football evidence predicts that, over time, you are more likely to score from this tactic of fully 'caging' a team in their own defensive third than you are to concede a counter-attack that leads to a goal.

Whilst using a +1 rest defence may be common, it is not bulletproof. Once the ball is moving, players are moving, and often untracked opposition forward runs might create numerical equality or even lead to moments of numbers-down as the opponent counter-attacks.

Transition to Attack (Winning the Ball)

Different teams have contrasting ideas of what actions they should complete with the ball once they regain it. There is a sliding scale between attacking directly at any given opportunity versus securing the ball and re-building an attack. These decisions relate to risk and reward (if we attack quickly and immediately, is the risk of doing so worth the higher likelihood of losing the ball?). Other BOTSS also impact these decisions.

Counter-attacking scenarios are again moments where numerical equality is seen as advantageous, and usually involves a team with high momentum moving forward against a retreating or recovering backline. Getting players into dangerous goal-scoring positions – before defenders have the chance to recover – is the essence of successful counter-attacking.

TACTICAL TASK 19

RECALL TASK 18 ABOVE. KNOWING MORE ABOUT DYNAMIC NUMERICAL SUPERIORITY, WHAT AREAS OF THE PITCH WILL YOU MOVE PLAYERS INTO (AND FROM) TO GAIN ADVANTAGES FOR YOUR TEAM?

Conclusion

Numbers, put simply, affect every part of the game. From situations that are static to those that are dynamic and changeable; from being unopposed to being numbers-up or numbers-down in certain situations; from 1v1 to 11v11 and all the combinations in between.

Numbers are, however, just the starting point when it comes to superiorities.

TACTICAL TASK 20 – LIGHTBULB MOMENT

WHAT WAS YOUR GREATEST LIGHTBULB MOMENT FROM THIS CHAPTER?

HOW CAN YOU IMPROVE YOUR UNDERSTANDING OF THIS IDEA?

Qualitative Superiority
We Have Better Players Than You

TACTICAL TASK 21

HYPOTHETICALLY:

WHAT MAKES ONE PLAYER BETTER THAN ANOTHER?

WHAT MAKES ONE TEAM BETTER THAN ANOTHER?

I have intentionally started this conversation around *qualitative superiority* in football with some questions and a task. On the surface, the questions might seem quite easy to answer – the better team is the team that wins, for example. So, if your approach to the task above was to answer in this short form, let's go on a journey together to really develop this answer and understand what 'better' in football actually is.

Understanding 'Better'

It seems like a war has raged in football for a long time and will continue to be fought forever. Who is better – Lionel Messi or Cristiano Ronaldo? For context, I will tell you now that I have a preference for one, probably just like everyone else, but I am certainly not going to get into an argument about it – although I do want to explore it! I have no interest in finding any final answer – I have already acknowledged that there is no logical, concrete one. It is not a maths problem with one formula that arrives at a decision. In fact, because of the duration of this debate, and the fact that nobody can ever be conclusively correct, I am quite bored of it, but I do want to use it as a vehicle to help us all understand what 'better' is or may be in football terms.

Messi? Ronaldo?

First of all, both players in this debate are *reasonably* easy to compare in some ways. They are both more-or-less the same age, they played during the same generation, and they were both attacking players, starting as wide attackers before playing more centrally, with a huge number of goals and assists. Throughout their playing days, they were in direct competition with each other whilst playing in Spain at the same time, before joining powerhouse clubs outside Spain (Paris Saint-Germain and Juventus, respectively) before moving to leagues that most would consider to be outside the traditional big leagues – in the US and Saudi Arabia.

In deciding who is better, we may be able to compare apples with apples. It is not like we are trying to compare them against other recent Ballon d'Or winners: Rodri, Modric – or even Benzema and the Brazilian attacking midfielder Kaká, who were the last two attacking players to win the award outside of Messi and Ronaldo. If we were to bundle all the six players mentioned above, we would probably conclude that, in their prime, Messi and Ronaldo were more similar in playing profile than any other pairing. And, despite their superstardom now, both were shy young players who blossomed into icons.

In many ways, however, the pair were also very different. Physically, Messi looked like a boy; Ronaldo, a machine. As many people argue, Messi was 'born with it' – he just needed the environment (and growth hormones) to allow him to flourish. Ronaldo was built and developed into a monstrous footballer in the gym and on the training pitch – and with ferocious ambition.

The thought of both of them playing in the same team in their pomp and at their brilliant best must now be left to our imagination. Maybe a charity game or some promo event will see them line up together when their careers end. However, I am unsure if they would have worked in the same team, even considering their qualitative awesomeness. I am confident that, psychologically, one of them would probably have needed to cede priority to the other, something that would have been unthinkable, a concept we look at in the upcoming chapter on *Cooperative Superiority*.

Comparing Footballers – Apples and Oranges

Whilst football's long-standing Messi-Ronaldo debate is still alive and breathing, we must understand that the only reason we would ever *actually need* to compare them closely (in a tactical sense, not as fans) would be if we were a Head Coach or club chairman that intended to sign one or the other – or a club that intended to play them together.

When you think about it, in competitive or game situations, whether *your* attacker is better than *their* attacker is almost a moot point. It matters to pundits as they can hypothesise the potential winning team being the one whose superstar performs best, but from a tactical planning point of view, the coach will prepare differently.

Instead, the coach will compare their attacker with your defender(s) and vice versa to assess the advantage(s) they might or might not have over each other. We *can* compare Robert Lewandowski to Erling Haaland to determine who we think is the better striker and why. However, if Barcelona were to play Manchester City, it would be much more useful to compare the Polish striker with City's centre-backs if we were going to achieve any real tactical advantage. The media may pitch the game as a battle of the world's top number 9s, but in essence it won't be. Or, thinking about it in another way, golfer X may play against golfer Y, but ultimately they don't affect each other's performance. If golfer X performs significantly better over 18 holes, he probably wins.[15] If Haaland performs significantly better than Lewandowski in the match, you could expect Manchester City to win.

---

[15] You will notice a lot of uncertain or uncommitted language here – "probably", "may" etc. This is something we should understand better in football. After all, if you pick up any football book based on logic, data, numbers, etc, they will all tell you that luck and chance always play an active role in the outcome of football matches.

So, in the real world and our tactical preparation of games etc., we cannot compare like-for-like in the hope of achieving qualitative advantages. We have to compare 'better' in a much more 'adjusted' way. If I am preparing to play against Messi, I don't counter that threat by asking Ronaldo to play better; I counter it by focusing on my defender and midfielders. As Jose Mourinho once noted, you need a "cage" or "jail" of players to defend against Messi, so their numerical superiority would be advantageous over his qualitative superiority. The Portuguese coach would literally set out to box him in, and gave all the players in his zone a share of defensive responsibility against the diminutive Argentine.

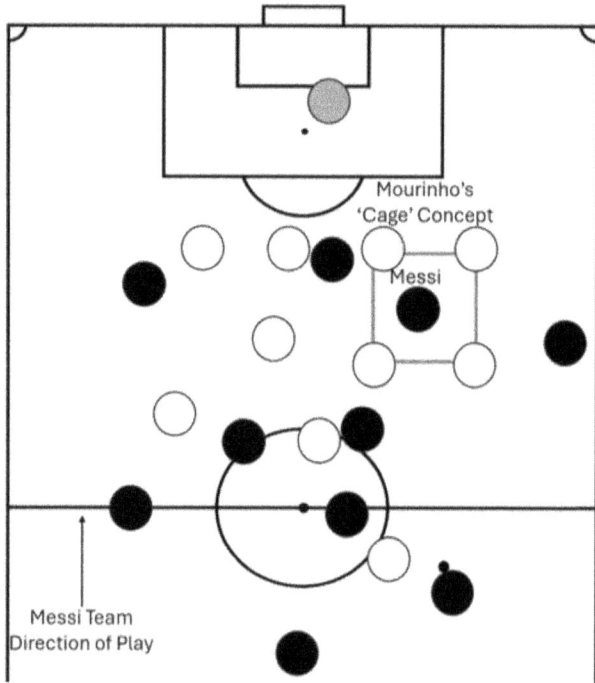

The cage idea used by Jose Mourinho to control the qualitative ability of Lionel Messi

> ## TACTICAL TASK 22
>
>
>
> **IF YOU ARE PREPARING A GAME AGAINST A TEAM WITH ONE PLAYER WHO HAS A PARTICULARLY QUALITATIVE STRENGTH, HOW WOULD YOU SET UP TO COMBAT IT? TRY TO ANSWER BASED ON THE REALITY OF THE BEST PLAYER(S) IN YOUR LEAGUE.**

Returning to our hypothetical Barcelona vs Manchester City match, let's say we decide that Lewandowski is a 'better' striker than John Stones is a defender, but we decide that he is a 'poorer' attacker than Ruben Dias is a centre-back. We now have some usable info.

If we just played the numerical game, we would conclude that the striker (Lewandowski) is certainly not better than *both* those centre-backs put together, but that is the picture we put attackers into week-in and week-out. Numerical superiority tells us we need support – a second striker, or the dynamic movements of a winger or attacking midfielder – to join him and create 2v2+ situations.

However, Lewandowski – and all other numerically disadvantaged attackers – have an inherent advantage over defenders; their quality is more valuable. If (and this is certainly true around the penalty box) a centre-back goes into a duel with a striker ten times, they need to win the vast majority of these duels. If they don't, the chance of conceding a goal or a big chance is higher. Strikers don't need to be better than defenders every time, just sometimes, maybe even just once. Things, however, swing back into the favour of the centre-back when we consider that the striker must ensure the ball ends up within the frame of a 24x8 foot goal, normally with a goalkeeper and a covering defence to beat, too. A defender can be successful (at the defending-only part), you could argue, if the ball ends up anywhere else! You can set up the strongest cage around Messi, but if he successfully wriggles free on just a couple of occasions, he could win the game!

All of this, then, leads us to other questions. If a striker scores, can the defender be considered to have had a good game? I assume most coaches would say yes, but what if the attacker scores two or three goals? If the striker doesn't score, can *they* be considered to have had a good game? And, if so, what other ways can a striker show his qualities? The list could go on and on.

I don't have readymade answers to all these questions. Football is so interesting and explorative because we need further context to come to any conclusions.

Probably the best conclusion we might have is to analyse performances over time. If a striker profiles as the team's goalscorer, we can judge them by their goal count over 20 games, two seasons, five seasons, etc., rather than just one game or one half. In the same way, we might judge defenders and goalkeepers, albeit in a very surface-level way, by clean sheets (more on this later!). We now also have access to a ton of other data points that will help us make these assessments. Websites and apps like WhoScored.com use data formulas to assess and give a tangible score and rating to players after games, then average them over time.

The journey does not end there, however. Attackers are not 'just' attackers. Defenders are not just 'defenders' – we have the opposite to consider, too! Is John Stones a better in-possession player than Robert Lewandowski is a defender? If Stones and Dias combined can be assumed to be considerably better with the ball than the Pole is without it, what should his defensive duties entail? What dynamic effect should that have on his teammates? In this game, should the striker prioritise stopping those players progressing the ball forward rather than pressing aggressively? If there is a moment where he notices a trigger to go and press, he will need his teammates to press with him so he is not outnumbered for long. But, again, you can say that the attacker has certain advantages. He only needs to win or intercept one poor technical action from either player to potentially bear down on goal. Stones and Dias need to be consistently strong in possession of the ball, and also in those moments when the ball is lost.

Ultimately, being 'better' is a complex calculation into the dynamic nature of the game. Whenever you are sure about something, an argument can be made against it.

Attributes

To gain more clarity and control over these ideas (after all, football tactics are basically a way for your team to try to control what will happen in a game), we can break attributes down into components.

Long Term Player Development (LTPD) Model Widely used across soccer and sport	
Technical Tactical	Psychological
Physical	Social

Earlier in this book, we looked at the often-used *Long Term Player Development Model* within football coaching. In the same way that we may use this model when talking about player development or team selection, we can also talk about it here.

When seeking qualitative advantages in football, we can use this model to identify and then utilise the stand-out qualities of individuals, units, or teams over the opposition.

Technical-Tactical Superiority Examples		
Individual (1v1)	*Unit*	*Team*
If I get Lionel Messi 1v1 against most defenders, we will be in an advantageous situation.	The dominant ball-possession midfield trio of Barcelona that featured Busquets, Xavi, and Iniesta.	The Real Madrid team under Zinedine Zidane that won the UEFA Champions League three times in a row.
If, however, Antonio Rudiger is competing in an aerial duel with Messi, the German will have the qualitative advantage.	Chelsea's defensive unit that conceded only 15 goals in the entirety of the 2004/05 Premier League season.	The Red Bull clubs that attack, defend, and transition with youthful energy and directness.

Physical Superiority Examples		
Individual (1v1)	*Unit*	*Team*
Utilising the height of Peter Crouch to win aerial duels.	British coach Tony Pulis was famous for playing with a defensive line of four tall centre-backs to add extra power and height to his team.	A 2023 CIES analysis of team height in football showed Hungarian side Kecskeméti TE to have an average height of almost 6 foot 2 inches!
Utilising the speed of Killian Mbappe to isolate slower defenders and hurt defences.	The stamina-based midfield trio of Henderson, Fabinho, and Wijnaldum that allowed Liverpool's attackers to thrive under Jürgen Klopp.	AC Milan's famous use of their on-site performance lab, Milanello, to extend the high-performance playing ages of their team.

Psychological Superiority Examples		
Individual (1v1)	*Unit*	*Team*
Thierry Henry and Cole Palmer's composure when 1v1 with goalkeepers.	The confidence of the Spanish National Team's defenders to take the ball from the goalkeeper and build from the back in major international tournaments.	Alex Ferguson's never-say-die attitude of his Manchester United treble-winners in 1998/99.
David Beckham's reliability and mental stability when taking important set-pieces.	The courage of title-winning midfield pairing Ngolo Kante and Danny Drinkwater to play effectively in their system, despite other inferiorities.	The willingness of teams like Brentford to attack corners with all 10 outfield players in / around the opponent's box

Social Superiority Examples		
Individual (1v1)	*Unit*	*Team*
Allowing creative individual players (Hazard, Messi, Ronaldo, Salah) to defend less to utilise their energy more in attack.	The core of Spanish and German National Team players from Barcelona and Bayern Munich that won the 2010 and 2014 World Cups, respectively.	The Celtic team of 1967 that won the European Cup with a team based entirely of players born within 30 miles of the club.
The trust that goalkeeper Ederson has from his teammates to produce Cruyff turns on his own goal line!	The synchronisation of Aston Villa's back line when executing successful offside traps.	The famous Wimbledon 'Crazy Gang' of the late 80s that used their team spirit and culture to their advantage.

With these examples in mind, let's go on a journey through football to understand qualitative superiority in individual, unit, and team ways.

1v1

The most commonly cited strategy to attain qualitative superiority in football matches is through individuals in 1v1 match-ups where one player has a superior attribute (of some variety) over their immediate opponent, just like those examples above.

Typically, the easiest example to bed in the idea is by hypothesising 1v1 duels between a winger and a full-back. Indeed, being excellent in 1v1 situations is probably the most prized asset for these players – both from attacking and defensive points of view, depending on the profile of the player.

One of the most calculated ways that teams create advantageous 1v1 attacking situations with wide attackers is through what is called 'overload to isolate'. The basic premise is that the team in possession will set up an attack with numbers down one side of the pitch, therefore dragging defensive attention to that side, before switching the ball to the opposite side to 'isolate' a defender 1v1 against a dangerous, qualitatively strong, wide attacker. Many of the best possession teams may even keep the ball for an extra few passes in the overload area to attract even more defensive cover to that side, to further increase the space for their 1v1.

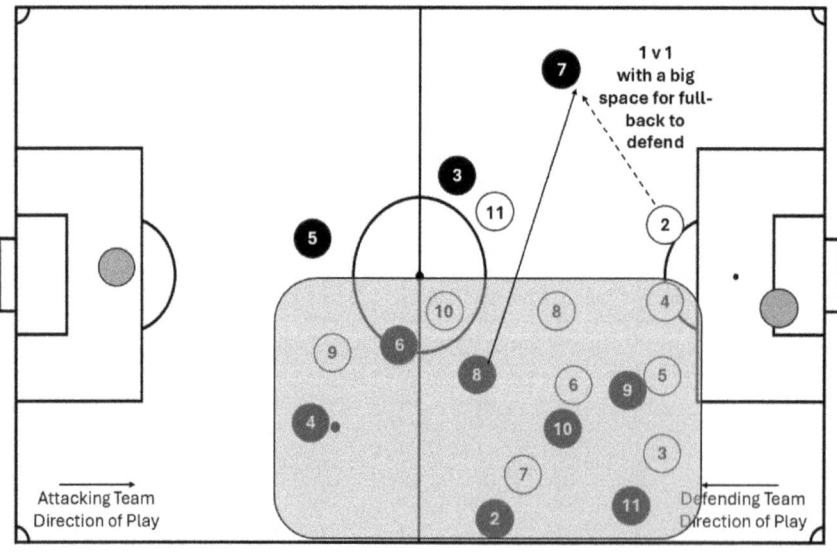

The blacks overload their right-hand side to drag opposition defenders to this part of the field, then quickly switch the play to create a 1v1 with their winger against the opposition full-back.

> **TACTICAL TASK 23**
>
>
>
> **IF YOUR TEAM WAS TO UTILISE THE 'OVERLOAD TO ISOLATE' CONCEPT, WHO IN YOUR TEAM WOULD YOU PREFER TO HAVE AS YOUR ATTACKER IN THIS SITUATION? HOW CAN YOU GET THEM INTO ADVANTAGEOUS 1V1 SITUATIONS LIKE THIS MORE?**
>
> **CONVERSELY, IF YOUR FULL-BACK GETS ISOLATED LIKE THIS, WHAT CAN YOU DO TO HELP?**

The rate and value of one player's success over the other is crucial. For example, in an isolated 1v1 situation, how often will the winger be able to take advantage of the circumstances compared to the full-back? What will the measure of success be? Maybe the creation of one goal outweighs five 'failed' attempts at making this advantage successful.

It *is* worth noting that there is no golden rule that states that *every* winger will be qualitatively better than the full-back in this type of situation. They certainly will not be successful in *every* duel, nor should we expect them to be. The duels that the winger is successful in, however, may have their team bearing down on goal.

Lots of other dynamic factors will come into play that will judge this as a successful tactic or not – even *Game State* factors will influence the duel. If it is late in the game and the black team needs to score, then maybe the winger will be more direct and take more risks to beat the full-back, etc. The quality of the pass to the winger will affect the outcome, as will the speed (or lack of) with which the overdrawn defensive cover recovers to help the full-back, for example. There is a before and after to every duel.

Within coaching, there is a tendency for 1v1 exercises to focus on the 'during' part of the skill alone. However, we must consider what happens both before and after the duel. How does a player move to receive the ball, and how does their teammate find them *before* the duel? Afterwards, what is the end product – a pass, a cross, a shot? Maybe it's a failure and a need to transition to defending? We all know those wingers who are devastating *during* the 1v1, but who lack the quality to produce a good end product *after* the duel.

Not all 1v1s are the Same

1v1 duels are not just a matter of Player A with the ball facing up against Player B without the ball. The graphic below, adapted from an Academy document from Michael Beale, shows the variants in these situations.[16] Furthermore, we can then add dynamic factors to the situation, which may include everything from where the duel is taking place on the pitch, to the amount of space available when the duel is afoot, to whether the ball in contest is on the ground, in the air, bouncing, spinning, etc. Having players who excel in these situations is very much a qualitative superiority for your team.

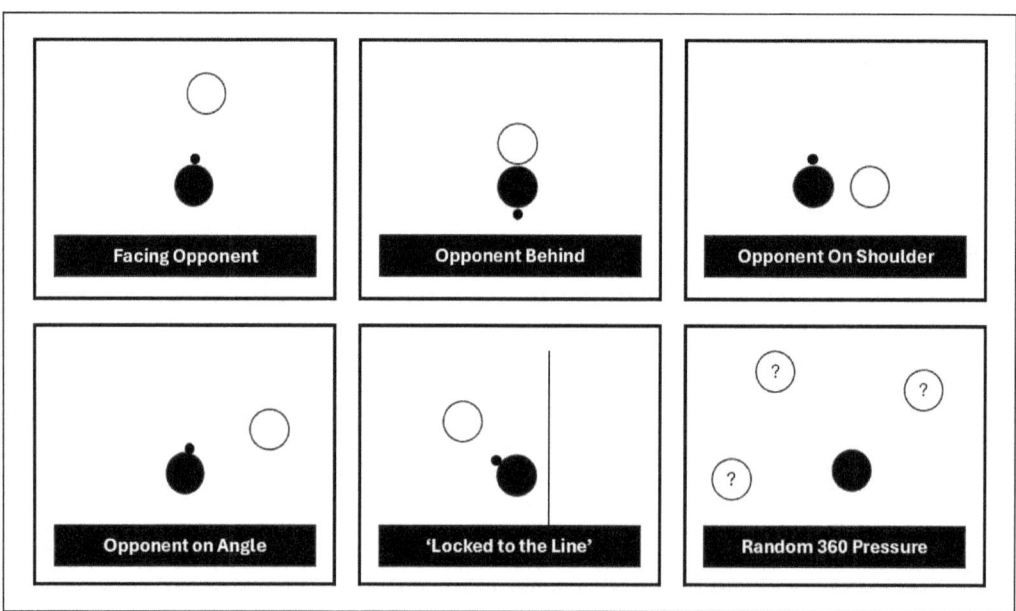

Michael Beale's different types of 1v1 scenarios

---

[16] We can even increase this by talking about 1v1 duels that will be contested aerially, or even the 1v1 where the successful player may only be able to use one touch – a clearance or a shot at goal for example; a deflection that takes a loose ball into the path of a team, or into space, etc.

Being Superior 1v1 Defensively Wins Games Too

It is a prize in itself for an attacker to complete a dribble against Netherlands defender Virgil van Dijk, such is the centre-back's composure in these situations. He rarely jumps into tackles and prioritises delaying attackers who may be attempting to run at him. In other 1v1 situations, he is an expert defender when "forechecking" – a term used by Jesse Marsch, and acquired from ice hockey – to mean an aggressive press to regain the ball. If you want to defend with a high defensive line, having defenders who can defend big spaces 1v1, 2v2, etc., is very important.

Players who are excellent in 1v1 defensive scenarios, whether they are traditional defenders at full-back or centre-back, or whether they are forwards who press intelligently, or midfielders who may track a forward 'just in case', can be worth their weight in gold. The value of 1v1 attackers is often noted on the scoreboard, but success when 1v1 defending is somewhat like trying to prove a negative. We can rarely say that the reason for not conceding a goal was because of a successful press from the striker, for example. Of course, when closer to goal, emergency defending situations are easier to attribute as goal-saving, but they still don't mean as much to the casual viewer or pundit. As coaches, though, we must acknowledge that just because they are not counted on the scoreboard does not mean they don't count!

Goalkeepers

It has always been traditional lore that a good goalkeeper will get your team an extra X number of points per season. In the past, this was again somewhat like proving a negative. How can we count goals that were not scored?! This is why traditional awards, such as the Golden Glove, are given to the goalkeepers with the most clean sheets. This is worthwhile but slightly misleading, too, as the goalkeeper with the most clean sheets tends to also be from a stronger team with better qualitative defenders, and with better players in general who will spend more time attacking than defending.

Today, though, more and more data around goalkeepers, xG, shot quality, "post-shot xG", expected saves, etc., are presented to give us the impact of a goalkeeper's actions on the scoreline – of goals they could or should have conceded – but didn't.

In the 2023/24 Premier League season, José Sá of Wolverhampton Wanderers stood out with exceptional goalkeeping metrics. Although he conceded 57 goals and only kept four clean sheets, he was 'expected' to concede over 66 goals, given the measured quality of the shots he faced. This means Sá prevented about 9 goals more than anticipated, highlighting his significant shot-stopping abilities. It was, of course, a top-four goalkeeper, David Raya of Arsenal, who took home the Golden Glove for keeping the most clean sheets (16).

In contrast to Sá's heroics for Wolves, the combined numbers of the three goalkeepers who played for Nottingham Forest was vastly different. Data from the same season found that – between them – they had conceded a huge *18* more goals than they were expected to! As coaches the world over will attest to, poor goalkeeping performances can really undermine your team tactics. Goals can get conceded 'out of nothing' and frequent mistakes or underperformances are highlighted and targeted further by opponents. If the goalkeeper drops a cross, guess where the next cross or corner goes – right on top of them!

Capitalising on Weaknesses

Today, match and opposition analysts have a lot of responsibility and can provide a lot of feedback to coaches. Ultimately, however, what that opposition feedback often boils down to is identifying their potential *strengths and weaknesses*. This can be provided before the game, but it can also be assessed in real time during the game.

Identifying and targeting the weakest players or units within a team structure is a very strong way of achieving qualitative superiority over an opponent. In his brilliant book, *11v11 Tactical Games*, Michale Beale actually includes a game called 'Pressing Victim', and the premise of the game is to identify and target a player or a small number of players who may be qualitatively weak. This could be a right-footed centre-back that you force to play on their left, a technically poor midfielder that you press aggressively, or a small striker that you physically dominate. Many coaches will strategically set up pressing 'traps' to filter the ball to a specific area, intending to win it back where they are strong and the opponent is weak.

> ## TACTICAL TASK 24
>
>
>
> HOW CAN YOU USE THE IDEA OF TARGETING 'PRESSING' VICTIMS WITH YOUR TEAM?
>
> IF YOU HAVE SPECIFIC KNOWLEDGE OF THE TEAMS YOU PLAY BEFOREHAND, CAN YOU IDENTIFY THE MAIN VICTIMS DURING YOUR PREPARATION FOR EACH GAME?
>
> IF THE EXACT QUALITIES OF YOUR OPPONENT ARE UNKNOWN, CAN YOU ANALYSE WHO CAN BE YOUR PRESSING VICTIM IN REAL-TIME DURING THE GAME, OR HAVE A PLAN FOR TARGETING A SPECIFIC POSITION? THIS COULD BE, LIKE ABOVE, A DEEP MIDFIELDER OR A LEFT CENTRE-BACK WHO MAY WELL FREQUENTLY BE RIGHT-FOOTED, OR IT COULD BE THE DIRECT OPPONENT OF THE STRONGEST PRESSERS IN YOUR TEAM.
>
> IT COULD ALSO, OF COURSE, BE A MIX OF ALL THE POTENTIAL IDEAS ABOVE.

Of course, you will also need to be hyper-aware of your team's weaknesses. You need to hypothesise what you can do to protect those weaknesses and limit them from being targeted. This may be by strengthening the problem area with cover and numbers, changing the team's shape or formation, or working on the training pitch to improve certain qualitative aspects of certain players.

Units & Teams

In a post-match interview, Jürgen Klopp was asked about a mistake from one of his defenders that led to a goal. Whilst defending 1v1 in the box (putting pressure on the striker from behind), Joe Gomez was outsmarted and the striker got away from him to score. When asked about what the reporter saw as a clear mistake from Gomez, Klopp was quick to point out the role of the defender's teammates, believing that the centre-back should not be forced to defend 1v1 in the box for any longer than necessary. Your teammates are always needed.

When you think about the concept of numerical superiority that we studied in the last chapter, it is in itself an attempt to be *qualitatively* better than an opponent. Just like the example above, the longer Joe Gomez was isolated 1v1 in a dangerous part of the pitch, the more dangerous it became. This situation called for numerical help!

Seeking numerical advantage is a typical strategy when combatting qualitative disadvantage. It may be that turning a 2v2 midfield contest into a 3v2 in your favour will make you qualitatively better in midfield. So, let's first of all note that achieving superiority of numbers can also achieve a qualitative upper hand. If the quality of Team A and Team B is equal when 2v2, then turning it into 3v2 should make one team 'better'.

Boiling football down into 1v1s is nothing new, although very flawed. There are estimates that every football match has hundreds of these 1v1 confrontations that, of course, can vary heavily in terms of their significance. 1v1 midfield duels, for example, might only last a split second apiece, but there may be dozens in a match. In contrast, a striker going 1v1 against the goalkeeper happens less frequently but will likely be a more significant moment in the game.

The length of time these duels exist is highly dependent on the players around the 1v1 and the support play, game-understanding, and decision-making of teammates. If you consider the *overload to isolate* diagram earlier in the chapter, the support play available to both players is important. With the final third and goal under threat in this situation, the defensive team cannot allow this 1v1 to last any longer than needed before getting adequate cover to help. Not only does good cover give the ball carrier two barriers to beat, it also frees the first defender mentally and allows them to press more vigorously and take more risks to win the ball back. Without this cover, or when cover takes too long to arrive, the defender may be risk-averse and more intent to delay the attacker and thus defend in a more reactive than proactive manner. Or, as you will hear commentators say, "He backed off and backed off until it was too late!"

The potential support play options of the 'Black number 3' in the diagram are interesting, too. Do they overlap/underlap to support the winger, or do they risk condensing and killing the space when the player 'White 11' invariably tracks his run? Maybe the 1v1 is more advantageous, so they make a conscious effort to stay away from the immediate action and just support the play from behind – or simply provide cover for the team in case the full-back does indeed win the ball. For their 'during' to be successful, the 'after' does too, which requires teammates to make it to the box and join the attack.

These micro-decisions made by players will often boil down to the quality of the players involved – as well as the overall quality of the partnership or unit in question.

TACTICAL TASK 25

WHICH UNIT IS THE STRONGEST QUALITATIVE ONE IN YOUR TEAM? HOW CAN YOU GET THE BEST OUT OF THEM?

WHICH UNIT IN YOUR TEAM IS QUALITATIVELY THE POOREST? WHAT CAN YOU DO TO INCREASE THEIR LEVELS (E.G., DO YOU CHANGE FORMATION AND ADD ANOTHER PLAYER TO MAKE THE UNIT NUMERICALLY STRONGER? IF SO, WHERE DOES THIS LEAVE YOU WEAKER?).

Earlier in this chapter, I spoke briefly about websites such as *WhoScored.com*, which use data to grade the performances of players in matches – or over a series of matches and even seasons. Below, for example, is the 2021/22 *Europe's Top 5 Leagues Team of the Season*, and their associated average scores (out of 10). This was the same year that the player with the highest score, Karim Benzema, was awarded the Ballon d'Or at the UEFA Best Player in Europe awards, showing that there is certainly some symmetry between what the data people are seeing in the numbers and what the coaches, players and journalists are seeing with their eyes.

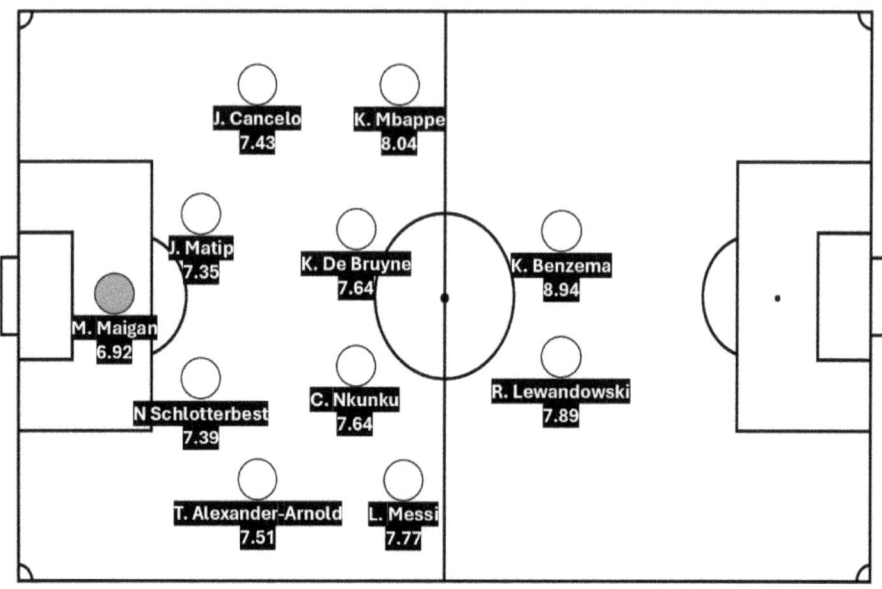

WhoScored.com 2021/22 Europe's Top 5 Leagues Team of the Season

It has not been lost on me, however, that the above features one of my pet hates – that of shoehorning players into non-preferred positions for the purposes of these hypothetical XIs. In my eyes (and you will read more about this in the chapter on *Cooperative Superiorities*), playing GK:4-4-2 where three of the four midfield line players are Neymar and Messi as wide midfielders, and Christopher Nkunku as a central midfield player would not even be hypothetically successful. We can then talk about how effective Kevin de Bruyne would be in a midfield when he is the most defensively balanced!

So, although this is data-generated and represents the best qualitative players, it is tactically flawed. It is imperative that you consider the qualities of your players, not just the quality of your players. According again to WhoScored's metrics, multi-purpose midfielders Ilkay Gündogan and Alex Witsel were two of the highest-scoring specialist midfield players in that season's Champions League with scores of 7.19 and 7.17, respectively. Whilst you can argue that both Lewandowski and Nkunku are qualitatively better than both midfielders, there is very little argument that their specialist midfield qualities would change the team (and the shape of the team) for the better.

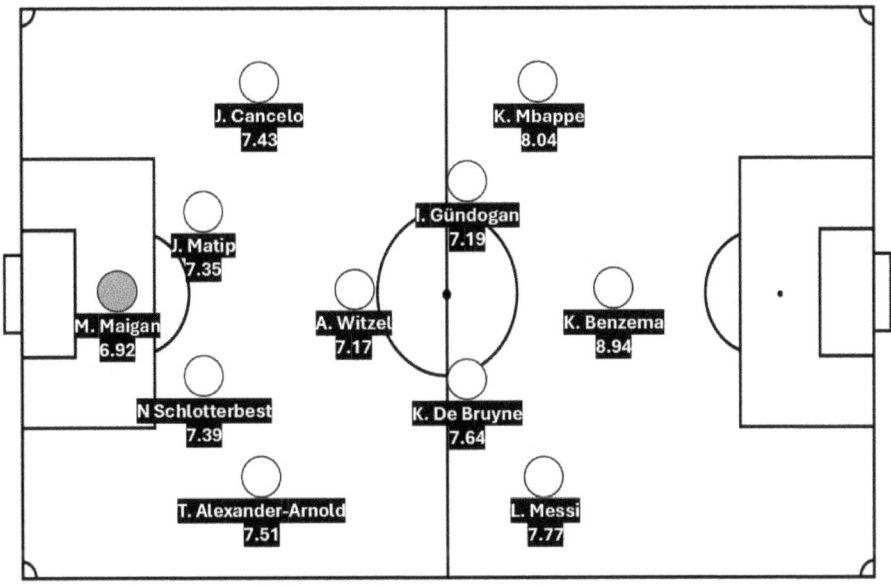

Player 'qualities' replacing player 'quality' to form a better functioning team

Whilst a hypothetical Best XI should not get my back up, it does! It does so in the same way when I watch match pundits dumb down the game on TV. I believe it works to downgrade the conversations the viewers, including coaches, will have around the game. I can guarantee you that should any of those 'midfielder' players above have seen this team, they would scoff and snigger at its validity, as its make-up simply does not constitute a team that has been constructed with realism in mind. If you played this 'Europe's Best XI' in a UEFA Champions League fixture, they may certainly win some – their quality ensures that – but they would, I am certain, be absolutely taken apart by any balanced, tactically well-setup football team at that level. The best teams have a balance of quality and qualities that allow them to function effectively across all four phases of the game.

Contrast the XI above with the Who Scored.com, Premier League Team of the Season accumulated eight weeks into the 2023/24 campaign. It shows an XI that, over time, could function and compete at the highest level of competition. It makes tactical and positional sense. Players have been selected based on their quality (their individual score) and their positional qualities, which include the roles and responsibilities they would be tasked to carry out. Players are not shoehorned into positions and roles that are flawed.

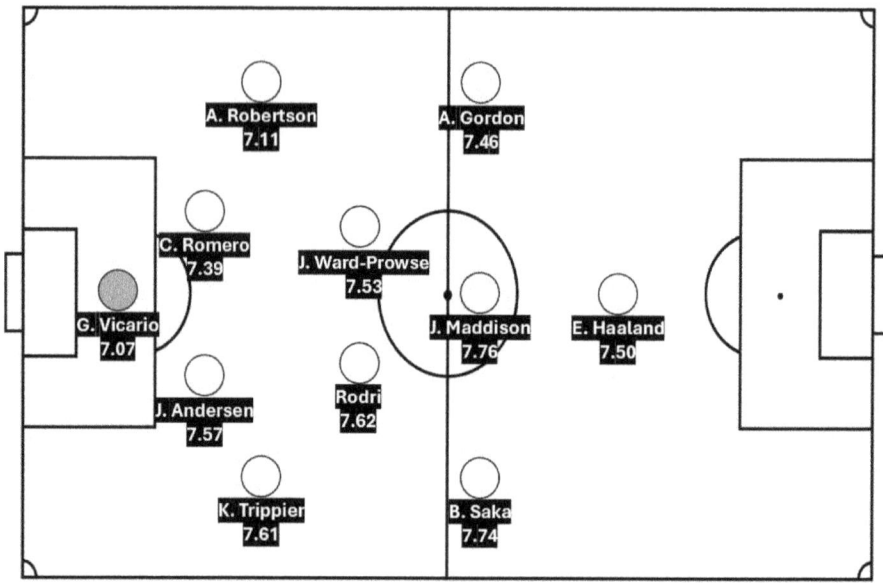

WhoScored.com Premier League Team of the Season ("So Far"[17]) 2023/24

Conclusion

The eleven best qualitative players should make a good team, but not always. There is a sweet spot between the quality of players and the way they work together. Often, when we pick the best 11 qualitative players, we abandon the balance between attacking and defending (and transitioning) that allows a team to function effectively.

In Soccer Tactics 2014, I wrote about the choices (and maybe even dilemmas) that coaches often face during team selection. At the time, this was based on Argentina trying to wedge attacking superstars Messi, Higuain, Aguero, di Maria, and Maxi Rodriguez (and defensive lynchpin Javier Mascherano) into the same team, which ultimately didn't work.

Below, I expand on the ideas from 2014, which still form the bedrock of choosing successful teams. Do you:

---

[17] Selected based on performances from August to October 2023.

1. Select the best 11 qualitative players and shape some sort of team formation and organisation around this, even if it means there is an attacking/defending imbalance? The quality may well ultimately trump all else.

2. Select a formation or style of play that you like as a coach, and then select the players that fit into this system? Which, of course, may mean leaving quality out of the team, which could even be your very best player (e.g., if your best player is a number 10, where would you include them to get their best version of themselves in a GK:4-3-3 formation?

3. Choose a mix of both 1 and 2, where you choose the formation and try to shoehorn the best players into that system (somewhat like the WhoScored team with Messi, Neymar, and Nkunku in a midfield four)?

4. Start with the selection of the one unit that you must play and build around that? I worked with a head coach who insisted on playing two strikers but did not want to play a traditional GK:4-4-2. We picked the front two then used the other players' strengths to pick and shape the rest of the team.

5. Assess the qualities of your players and how they may function together in their units (traditional and modern), and base your team shape and formation around these qualities? If you have an excellent number 10, play a formation that allows them to excel, with players around that will help them shine. If you have three excellent centre-backs, play a three-at-the-back formation. If you don't have good wingers, play a system without wingers. If you have a qualitatively poor defensive line, select players in the back line with some qualities (e.g., speed) and choose to play with a backline of five to add numbers or an excellent midfield screener to lessen the quality problem.

6. Mix all these options at different times?

TACTICAL TASK 26

WHAT TEAM-SELECTION APPROACH DO YOU USE? INVESTIGATE WHY THIS IS.

IS THERE AN APPROACH YOU LEAST PREFER? IF SO, HYPOTHESISE WHY IT MAY BENEFIT YOU OR YOUR TEAM TO DO SO (EVEN IF JUST TO GIVE YOU AND YOUR PLAYERS A DEVELOPMENTAL CHALLENGE).

Remember, the dynamism (and luck!) of football always plays a part in the outcome of any game. In qualitative terms. it may be advantageous that you gain in 1v1, unit, or whole-term stages that may contribute to winning or losing. However, you may even be qualitatively superior in many of these areas and still lose! We cannot control all of the outcomes – and relying on the ball hitting the net at one end and not at the other is tough. What we aim to achieve with tactics is to control the direction of travel towards those outcomes that help us win or lose.

TACTICAL TASK 27 – LIGHTBULB MOMENT

WHAT WAS YOUR GREATEST LIGHTBULB MOMENT FROM THIS CHAPTER? HOW CAN YOU IMPROVE YOUR UNDERSTANDING OF THIS IDEA?

Positional Superiority

Our Players are Better Positioned than Yours

When I submitted the first draft of this chapter for review, one particular response I got went something along the lines of "Hmmm… I was expecting it to be about positions – like, playing positions. You know, as in our defensive midfielder is better than your defensive midfielder at being a defensive midfielder…" and so on. So, I am therefore shoehorning in an early idea of what *Positional Superiority* is not, before we start in earnest! It is not about one specific playing position or positional unit. It is not about a striker being better than the other striker, etc.

It *is* about two sets of players duelling over occupation for the best spaces on the pitch – and then who will occupy them, how they will occupy them, and for what reason. These positional advantages will be momentary, and their success will often come down to the minute decisions of an individual player. Some of these spaces are more valuable than others, although this value changes at different times, as we will explore throughout.

TACTICAL TASK 28

TAKE A LOOK AT THE PITCH BELOW. WHICH TEAM WOULD YOU PREFER TO BE IN THAT MOMENT? PLEASE CONSIDER THE BARE FACTS AND ONLY THE INFORMATION YOU HAVE (2 V 3+GK, THE TWO ATTACKERS IN POSSESSION OF THE BALL NEAR THE HALFWAY LINE).

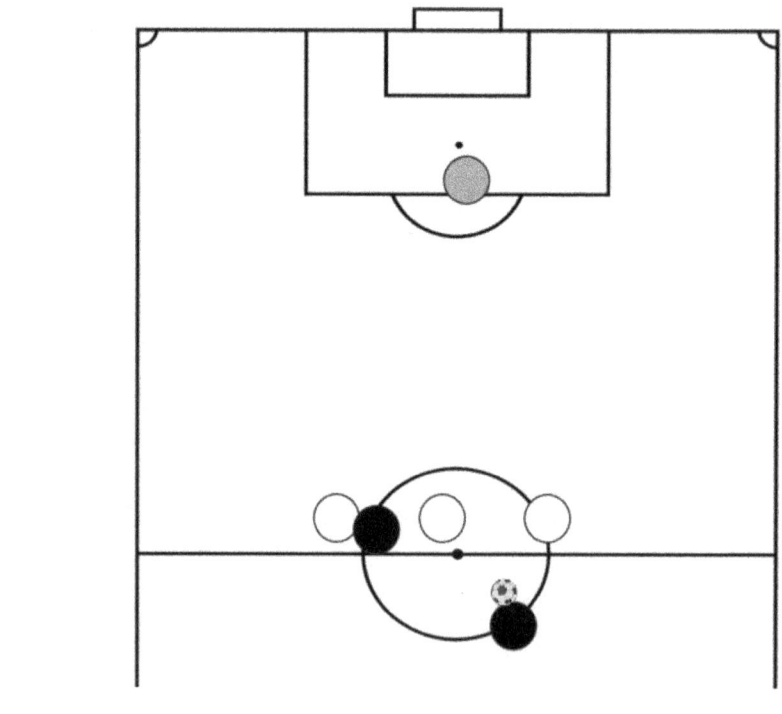

I assume the short answer to the task above will be that you would prefer to be in the situation of the team in black – even despite what some conventional wisdom of the other superiorities might say. The black team are numerically disadvantaged, and the whites are certainly compact. The blacks are still half a pitch from goal and must also consider the obstacle of the goalkeeper to ultimately turn this situation into a goal.

Of course, if we 'un-pause' the snapshot of the game above, we can start to factor in what role recovering defenders and black teammates joining the attack might undertake. We would also be able to see further nuance around the exact body shape of the defenders and, of course, the qualitative levels of all the players involved.

The major advantage that the black team has is *positional*. The player in possession of the ball is *between the lines* (behind the midfield and in front of the defence), facing forward and without immediate pressure. Their teammate is positioned *between* defenders and ready to dart forward into the space behind the three defenders, hoping for a direct, unimpeded run to goal.

Now, there is a lot of information we don't know, and we are making certain assumptions. Your striker may be especially slow, or the recovering defenders are quick, or the player in possession may be indecisive or lack composure, causing them to execute any pass or technical action poorly. However, if we assume that the players all play at the same age and level, the black team are poised to launch a dangerous attack.

This is the essence of positional superiority – can we get players into areas of the pitch that can hurt the opponent when in possession and in attacking transition, and can we dominate key areas without the ball and in defensive transition?

Pitch Control

Amidst the fight that is taking place for various superiorities during a football match, the one thing that will ebb and flow across the whole game is the physical areas of the pitch that each team can be considered 'dominant' or in control of. The ideas above have evolved into what is known as *Pitch Control*. At the professional level, this is the visualisation of a football pitch split into malleable physical zones, defined by which player from whichever team is 'controlling' them.

Traditionally, Voronoi diagrams, similar to the one below, were used to create a visual of an individual player's influence on the pitch. Creating a Voronoi diagram involves dividing the pitch into areas based on the positioning of players relative to each other, and relative to where the ball is.

For example, the goalkeeper (30) can be deemed to be in control of the large segment of the pitch that makes up all of the third that he is occupying, plus approximately 80% of his own half. In other words, he can hypothetically arrive at any point in that segment before an opposition player can. Striker number 9 is in control of the area that straddles a large portion of the centre-circle line in his own half.

Should player 5 receive the ball from player 45, who is currently in possession, he should have enough 360 degree pitch control to receive comfortably and have time and space to decide what happens in his next action.

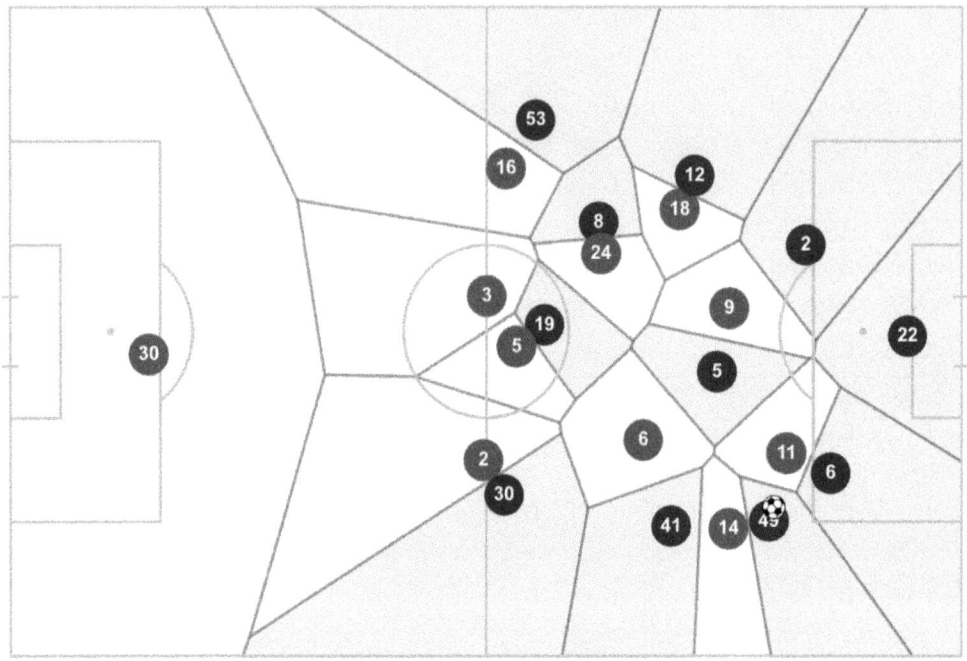

Diagram taken from www.footovision.com website and article: 'Visualizing positioning and player decisions: the innovation of Dynamic Pitch Control'

These diagrams, however, were found to have limitations. As mathematical models, Voronoi diagrams did not precisely consider enough traits of the individual players involved – like their speed, for example. In much the same way that some xG models do not factor in the ability of the shooter when making an expected goal calculation (i.e., they provide a data point based on 'averages' rather than specifics), early versions of Pitch Control were not specific enough either.

To address these shortcomings, William Spearman, Lead Data Scientist at Liverpool FC, developed the *Dynamic Pitch Control* model (where have we heard that *dynamic* word before!?). This model considers the dynamism of the game and evaluates how long it would take players to reach specific areas, providing a more accurate representation of control on the field. For example, if speedster Killian Mbappe is matched in a race with Jannik Vestergaard (the slowest player in the Premier League according to EA FC 25!), the model would give a great prediction in favour of the Frenchman getting there before the Dane. Other important details within the game – body position, direction of travel, movement factors in a specific moment, etc. – can now be factored in.

TACTICAL TASK 29

WHICH PLAYERS IN YOUR TEAM PROVIDE YOU WITH THE MOST PITCH CONTROL, MOST OFTEN? YOU DON'T NEED ACCESS TO A PITCH CONTROL DIAGRAM FOR THIS, JUST A SENSE OF WHICH PLAYERS DOMINATE THEIR IMMEDIATE SURROUNDINGS THE MOST.

WHAT PLAYERS STRUGGLE WITH ASPECTS OF PITCH CONTROL?

In Possession – The Most Advantageous Spaces

Football is hugely variable, but a certain amount of predictability is involved in our game, too. If you were to summarise football in its most simplistic way, you could say that two teams are fighting to score more goals than each other. To achieve this, there are key spaces on the pitch that, speaking in probabilities, need to be attacked and need to be defended.

The most advantageous spaces in terms of creating and scoring goals also need to be defended with the most conviction, making the same spaces important for both attacking and defending. These spaces are highlighted on the pitch map below.

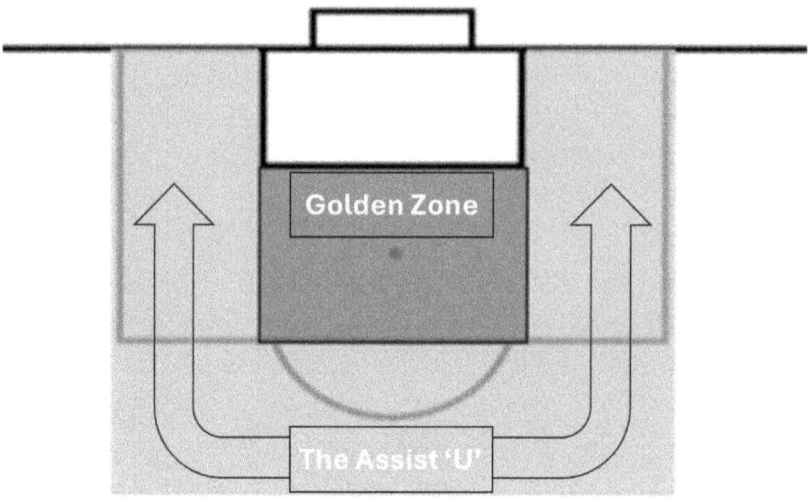

Where 80%+ of goals and assists come from

It shouldn't come as any surprise to anyone (but often does) that goals are scored and assisted in and around the penalty area – essentially the closest central spaces to the goal. If you were to take your favourite league and plot a season-long record of goals and assists on a pitch map, most people's maps would look eerily similar. Approximately 80-90% of goals in most leagues are scored with a final touch from the *Golden Zone*. Approximately 80-90% of assists will, in turn, come from what I have called the *Assist 'U'*.

You will quickly find information on the 'Golden Zone' within football research, as well as further detail about assists too. The assist research will point you in three broad directions… into an area that makes a 'U' shape around the golden zone:

- Zone 14
- The 'halfspaces'
- The wide channels inside the penalty area

Again, if we wanted to summarise football briefly, we could say that getting the ball into these assist areas and then getting it into the Golden Zone is the recipe for scoring goals and, therefore, the opposite is true when defending – keep the ball and the opponent away from these areas as much as possible.

The rest then – how to enter these areas and how to prevent entry into these areas – comes down to the coach. Longer passes and direct play can allow the *ball* to enter these areas more easily and more often, although being in control of the ball can be an issue as longer passes tend to be more difficult to control and can be pressurised much more easily. Other teams will be more patient in possession and look to enter less but enter with their team in charge of the ball and with a stronger probability of converting the attack into a goal. Some teams will choose to defend these areas by prioritising a low defensive block outside the penalty area, acting as a barrier to entry. Others will choose to prioritise defending as far away from their own goal as possible. The choice is yours.

TACTICAL TASK 30

HOW DOES YOUR TEAM PRIORITISE HOW IT ATTACKS AND DEFENDS THESE SITUATIONS? DIRECT PLAY? CLEAN BUILD-UP? HIGH, LOW, OR MID-BLOCKS? HIGH PRESSING? DELAY?

The Golden Zone

As per the diagram above, the 'Golden Zone' refers to the central area within the penalty box, between the six-yard and 18-yard lines, extending to the width of the six-yard box. This zone is considered the most effective for converting scoring opportunities due to its proximity to the goal and favourable shooting angles.

With all the data and sports science in football today, there is such a satisfying logic to goal-scoring. The final touch to goals comes from being as near to the goal as possible, without being 'too near' so that the goalkeeper can essentially control the immediate goalmouth. The vast majority of these shots are one- or two-touch finishes (as there is simply not enough time and space given to players positioned in such a dangerous area, so shots need to be taken quickly). Shots taken from this area are more likely to succeed due to their proximity to goal. Teams often structure their attacking play to arrive in this crucial area, utilising strategies like penetrative passing, intricate passing sequences, crosses and cutbacks, and well-timed off-the-ball movements to exploit this space effectively.

Zone 14

In football analytics, you sometimes see or hear of the pitch being divided into 18 squares or "zones" to facilitate game analysis and tactical planning (in all honesty, though, you very rarely hear of anyone talking about zones other than Zone 14). Among these, Zone 14 holds particular significance, playing a key role in creating and scoring goals. The logic continues when we take the goal-scoring narrative outside the Golden Zone. Data indicates that shots on goal from Zone 14 – the area centrally located just outside the penalty area – have a higher success rate compared to shots taken outside the box, again due to their central view of goal.

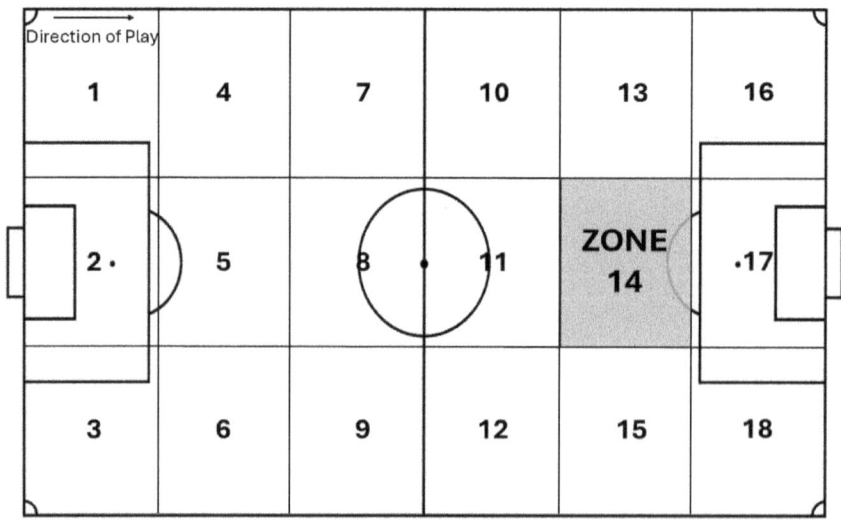

Zone 14

Statistical analysis has shown that a substantial percentage of goals are either assisted from or initiated in Zone 14. When a skilled player receives the ball in this space, they can quickly distribute it to various other attacking areas ahead of them, such as the wide areas, or directly into the penalty box – straight to the Golden Zone, or into the Golden Zone via the wide areas in the box.

Whilst assist numbers from this zone are high, the concept of the 'hockey assist' is also important when analysing Zone 14. In ice hockey, an assist is attributed to up to two players who contributed to a goal – the one with the final pass and the player before it. Applying this concept to football, a 'hockey assist' (sometimes known as a 'pre-assist' or 'secondary assist' in our sport, though rarely mentioned in conventional analysis) would recognise the player who makes the pass leading to the final assist.

Some brief research into football hockey assists showed the names you would expect to see. Players like Kevin de Bruyne, Neymar, Julian Brandt, Douglas Costa and Miralem Pjanić all featured positively in this much under-researched metric. When examining the top five European leagues in the 2017/18 season, Borussia Mönchengladbach's forward Lars Stindl stood out with 11 hockey assists, and it is fair to conclude that there is certainly a type of player who thrives in these 'Assist U' areas, namely a skilful, attack-minded technician.

The concept of hockey assists is particularly pertinent in Zone 14, where players often execute key passes from here that set up the final assist, contributing significantly to goal creation. Imagine a pass from Zone 14 to the wide channel for a winger to cross or cut back to a striker to score.

TACTICAL TASK 31

RESEARCH GOALS THAT HAVE BEEN SCORED IN THIS WAY – A HOCKEY-ASSIST FROM ZONE 14, OR AN ASSIST FROM A WIDE CHANNEL WITH A FINISH INSIDE THE BOX. USE YOUTUBE OR ANY GOAL FOOTAGE SOURCE.

Both attacking and defending strategies heavily emphasise control over this zone; attacking teams aim to exploit it to enhance their scoring potential, while defensive teams strive to limit the opponent's actions within this critical area.

The Halfspaces

In the early 2000s, football coaches did what football coaches do – they adapted and changed the game. With the growing influence of Zone 14 – and technical number 10s that were exploiting the zone that was frequently left vacant within GK:4-4-2 structures – coaches started to put one, then two defensive midfielders into their teams to shut its influence down. This ultimately led to the popularisation of the GK:4-2-3-1 formation as it gave a balance of defending this space with two defensive-minded midfield players and the offensive options of four attackers ahead of it.

Interestingly, it also led to players we may have profiled as 'traditional number 10s' being forced to play away from the central Zone 14 and into wider areas. Rather than being fixed to one position, these players drifted and *arrived into* key spaces, rather than being positioned there waiting. In turn, these attacking midfielders have become multi-functional and can usually play inside or outside the pitch – central or wide. You may often hear the term 'inside winger' (a player who plays between both the wide and inside channels), highlighting the merger of wingers and attacking midfielders in recent decades. This also highlights the increase in strategic value of the 'halfspace' as a key space through which to attack.

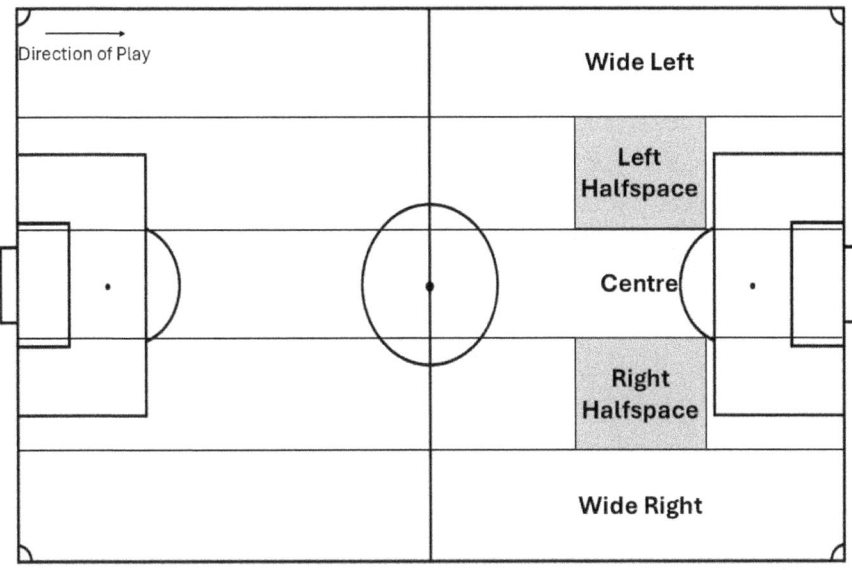

The Five Vertical Lanes

Certainly, a more common pitch division than the 18 zones is the use of the *Five Vertical Lanes* (they are called 'vertical' from the perspective of the players playing in the match; the term 'horizontal' is used to mean from side-to-side). Among these lanes, the "halfspaces" are the channels located between the central area and the wide areas on both sides of the field.

Although the lanes run the length of the pitch, it is most common to hear of the halfspaces being exploited (or defended) in the areas immediately either side of Zone 14, as shown above. The position of these zones and their rise in offensive popularity literally maps how defensive teams have tried to push attacks away from the centre, but attacking teams have refused to go all the way out wide!

These zones are crucial because they offer a balance between the central route to goal (which teams tend to block up) and the wider far-from-goal options provided by the more spacious flank areas. Gaining positional advantage in these halfspaces is very useful as it is away from the busy centre, but also gives the players 360-degree options that wide areas do not (due to the proximity of the touchline).

The strategic exploitation of halfspaces significantly impacts assistance and goal-scoring opportunities. Players operating in these areas can deliver diagonal passes into the goal area that are more challenging for defenders to intercept, increasing the likelihood of creating goal-scoring chances. For instance, midfielders like Kevin De Bruyne and full-backs like Trent Alexander-Arnold have excelled in exploiting halfspaces, often providing key passes that lead to assists. Teams such as Manchester City under Pep Guardiola have effectively employed tactics that emphasise halfspace occupation, resulting in a high number of assists originating from these zones. Research and data show that the halfspaces produce more forward passing than any other area of the pitch. By focusing on halfspace exploitation, teams can enhance their offensive efficiency, leading to an increase in good chances created, assists, and goals.

TACTICAL TASK 32

HOW CAN YOUR TEAM USE THE HALFSPACES MORE IN YOUR ATTACKING PLAY?

The Wide Channels Inside the Penalty Area

A natural extension to these halfspaces is the wide channels extending from the halfspace areas into the penalty box.

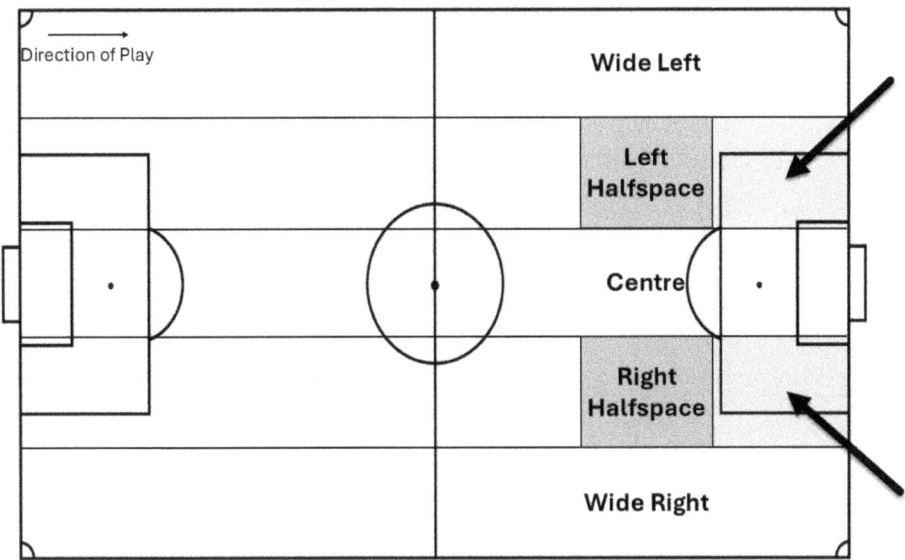

Again, when accounting for the advantages allowed by these spaces, football logic quickly takes over – they are closer to the goal and golden zone than the wide flank areas, but they are less busy than the centre. It is easier to penetrate these areas as the goalkeeper rarely gets involved in defending them (as opposed to playing a penetrative pass into the box centrally that can activate the goalkeeper to come out 'sweeping' to claim the ball).

They allow 'passes into the golden zone' rather than high crosses, which are more difficult to finish against two or three tall defenders. The exploitation of this space has led to an increase in goals scored from cutbacks and *low* crosses, unlike many predisposed ideas that assists from crosses usually come in the form of looping high crosses and towering headers (this does happen, but not as much as you might believe!).

TACTICAL TASK 33

HOW CAN YOU HELP YOUR TEAM TO ARRIVE IN THESE SPACES – THE GOLDEN ZONE AND THE ASSIST U – MORE?

A few times in this book, I have asked the reader to think about football in its most basic form, and I will come back to this idea here. The thought that football is a constant battle between one team looking to invade these pre-defined spaces around the penalty box, to deliver something clean to a goalscorer in a pre-defined golden zone, and the other team trying to prevent it, is classic invasion-game tactics. But what happens when these pre-defined spaces 'move'? The size and shape of the field of play will always be the same; the lines do not move mid-game, nor do the goals. What does move, however, are players whose dynamic movement and positioning somewhat reshape our interaction with the game.

Dynamic Spaces

Beneath the lights of the Camp Nou Stadium in Barcelona, the ball dropped to Chelsea left-back Ashley Cole in his penalty area, only a few yards from the penalty spot and 12 yards or so from his own goal line. Chelsea were under intense pressure from their Catalan rivals, who were chasing a much-needed goal in injury time of the Champions League semi-final. The ball is not clean, though, and a deflection cannons the ball into Cole's chest, who, to his credit, manages to somewhat control it before swinging his weaker right foot at it. He launches what rugby fans might call a 'garryowen' – a clearance that has more height than distance. It was very much a clearance that, seconds later, however, had turned into a famous assist. Fernando Torres, the only player wearing the white of Chelsea not actively defending the box, at that moment, latched onto the up-and-under from Cole, then ran half the length of the pitch before rounding goalkeeper Vitor Valdes to score.

Cole's position on the pitch is not typical of a space that would provide a high value for assists. However, it does highlight the dynamism of football. Depending on numerous variables, from the score line (Barcelona were attacking hard and taking risks in doing so) to the position of the opposition players (all outfield Barcelona players were in the final third) to the quality of the players (had that fallen to Cole's left foot, it was possible he would have connected with it better and the ball may have flown straight through to Valdes). Even the positioning of the goalkeeper and goalscorer was interesting. Torres was only beyond the last Barcelona defender as he had tried to run the ball out of danger seconds before, and the lack of an aggressive starting position from Valdez was unusual for such an eccentric goalkeeper. All these micro factors can make a macro difference. As soon as the commentary team realised that Torres was able to capitalise on this clearance, they knew that Barcelona's goal was under threat – even from the halfway line.

It is important, therefore, to note that no space on the field is always favourable for one team or another. There are certainly parts of the field that are more valuable more often, though.

Behind the Defence

The crucial reason for the success of the above Torres goal was the same as the famous goal the Spaniard scored in the 2008 European Championships Final against Germany, although they may 'feel' totally different to watch. Both goals saw Torres (and Chelsea and Spain) exploit the space behind the defensive line, which exposed the goalkeeper. Again, football logic is alive and well – if you can penetrate the last line of the opponent's defence, your scoring chances increase dramatically.

The space that teams can exploit behind the last line is different from the spaces we looked at above. This space is *dynamic* and will depend on the positioning of the opposition at a given moment. Conversely, teams are very adept at defending this space for obvious reasons. Whether that is when they are in low, mid, or high compact blocks, giving the opposition as little access to this space as possible is vital. In fact, the same principle exists regardless of your defensive philosophy – making sure that either your defenders or your goalkeeper are in 'control' of this space. If you quickly scan the *Pitch Control* map at the beginning of the chapter, you will see that both teams control the space behind the defensive line. *But* during those moments when it is penetrated, like with Torres above, with an exposed goalkeeper, it can be costly.

Playing Between and Behind the Lines

There is a reason why teams don't aim (or shouldn't aim) to attack the opponent 'in behind' each and every time they are in possession of the ball. This space, you can say, is difficult to access *cleanly* when you account for the superiorities that defensive lines have in these situations. For the most part, the defence will have a numerical advantage and will often have a physical, qualitative advantage – plus, they have the positional superiority of the defenders to block and intercept, *as well as* the goalkeeper to potentially sweep up any balls that do break through. This space is difficult to access due to a combination of pitch geography (think of the attacking team trying to play a pass into the space behind the defence and the ball running directly out of play) and defenders positioned to complete any defensive action necessary – including the action of the goalkeeper. Instead then of going directly in behind all of the time, teams and players look to access the space *in front of the defence*.

In the previous chapter, I shared the below graphic on Mourinho's 'cage' for Lionel Messi. This is a great example of a player achieving positional advantage. If we plot Messi's position on a Pitch Control map, he would 'own' a certain amount of the square in all four directions – in front of him, behind him and to both sides – and crucially he is occupying more than one opponent player whilst doing so.

In this situation, the Argentine is positioned 'between the lines'. Normally, this means that a player has taken up a position between the opposition's midfield and defending lines (although it can also mean finding a position between the opposition forward and midfield line).

The most successful players at exploiting these spaces tend to be the multi-functional or multi-positional attacking midfielders that we spoke about above, and there is certainly a variant of other full-backs, midfielders, and forwards who can operate successfully in these areas.

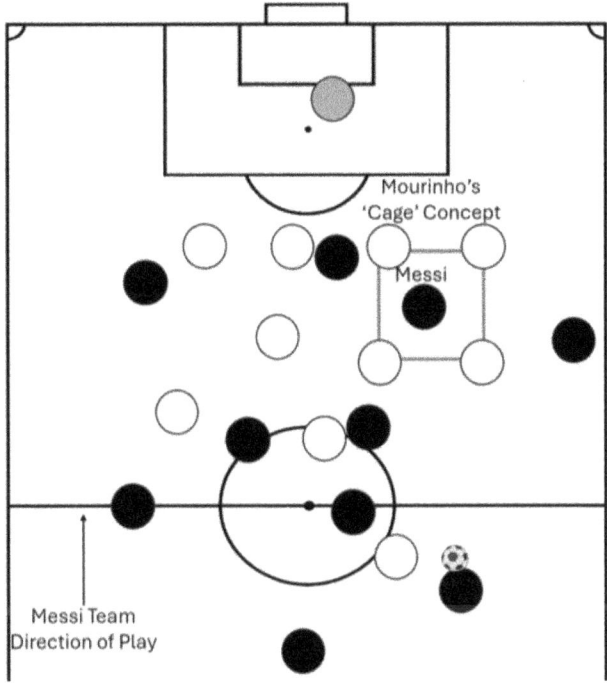

Between Defenders

Closely related to the concept of receiving between the lines are players taking up positions and receiving *between defenders*. This would be situations where a player utilises a gap or a 'pocket' to gain an advantage for the team. This could be between or behind two players or more, on the 'blindside' of an opponent (a spot where the opponent just cannot see them), or just in a position where defenders find it hard to get to them immediately.

One of the most basic individual defensive attributes is marking – and it is potentially the first thing many players will learn about defending when they are young. The centre-back will mark the centre-forward, the defensive midfielder will mark the number 10, etc. This, for a start, is a little old school, whilst not completely out of date. Marking (certainly player-to-player marking) and defending is more of a collective effort than following your player around all game.

This marking is generally instigated by the team who is out of possession (clearly!). The opponent has the ball, so we will defend and mark the key players who may pose a threat to our goal and goal area. What you see sometimes, however, is attacking or in-possession players essentially marking the defender. In other words, they position themselves at a disadvantage. It is like they are so used to hearing that X and Y are direct opponents that they enter this close-quarters duel too early. The outcome is that every time they become active in the play, the defender has positional advantage. In-possession players should, therefore, focus their off-the-ball energy on finding spots and positions *away* from opposition defenders, or try to enter spaces that defenders don't want to go. One particular training game I like to play is to make certain players wear a tag hanging from their back (the sort you see in tag rugby), and if they are 'tagged' off-the-ball, they must freeze for 10 seconds. This leads them to actively change their positioning to be away from defenders, but interestingly, they also change the position of their body (i.e., their body orientation).

TACTICAL TASK 34

CHART HOW OFTEN YOUR TEAM WILL PRIORITISE PLAYING IN BEHIND THE LINES, COMPARED TO PLAYING BETWEEN THE LINES.

Individual Positional Superiority

For a team to take advantage of all these above spaces – both the fixed and dynamic ones – we will also need to develop the ability and game sense of individual players. A player's ability to consistently receive the ball in advantageous spaces, making it easier for their team to progress the play and create goal-scoring opportunities, makes them an exceptionally valuable member of the team and squad.

A player's success in this respect will come down to many things, but to achieve it consistently, over time, players need a combination of skills.

Scanning – Awareness

The word 'scanning' is used so much in football now that maybe it's starting to lose its punch. As coaches or players, we often hear the word and assume we already have a concept of it. Many believe that scanning is best defined by these great big head swings, where you 'check your shoulders'. Scanning, however, is simply about awareness. Checking shoulders is absolutely fine, but you must be adding information – there is a defender there, a full-back out of possession, space there, a teammate over there, etc. This can be done with big scans, but it can also be done with 'micro-scans' or shorter 'rapid eye movements'. For the casual viewer, this is easiest to see, for example, shortly before a player takes a free-kick. Their eyes quickly scan the penalty box for any information they need. Players can also do this in-game; we just don't get the opportunity to see it.

A player cannot take advantage of space unless they know where the space is, how long it has been open, when it is likely to close up again, and when they need to arrive in it for it to be advantageous. Plus countless other little considerations. Can *that* teammate find me with the pass if I go there? Will *that* opponent be better qualitatively once I am in there? Etc. Players will not, of course, consciously ask these questions, but the best ones will have automatic thought processes like these. This is where instinct, match experience, and game sense (all trained over time) kick in.

Body Orientation

Much like scanning – and connected to the ability to scan proficiently – good body orientation or body 'shape' is something that is prescribed by coaches a lot and is infuriating when players don't develop this habit. Scanning and body shape are intrinsically linked. If you scan well, you will know how to position your body optimally. If you position your body well, you can see more and therefore become more aware of what you should or should not do in certain situations.

Body orientation refers to how a player positions their body relative to the field, teammates, and opponents, and this is normally done in a 'side-on' manner, much like when you cross the street. You cross the street safely by scanning left and right, but only because your body is orientated for you to do so swiftly and easily. If you are crossing a busy road, you would not do so facing the wrong way. If you are to receive a forward pass in a position between the lines, it is much better to be already facing forward or half-open, to be able to face and move forward quickly.

There is no use in finding pockets of space between the lines if your body orientation is forcing you backwards, or you will lose vital seconds when looking to turn. Some coaches will use key phrases to help players develop this body shape habit – the need to "see both goals", for example, that triggers a body shape that is side on.

Individual Off-the-Ball Movement

By using scanning and body shape, we can then start to identify those positions we need to receive the ball. Finding the spaces we spoke about (above) where you are free, even for a moment, and ideally facing forward or side-on, makes receiving the ball easier before we get to the final part – capitalising on your positioning and exploiting defensive gaps. Intelligent movement also has a knock-on effect. As we saw in the previous chapter, with the *overload to isolate* concept, defenders can over-compensate for good movement and positioning, thus leaving spaces and players free elsewhere.

In Germany, Thomas Müller is known as the "raumdeuter", which literally translates as "space finder". One of Bayern Munich and Germany's most prized players got to this stage by learning the timing of movement. After all, it is not the space that hurts opponents; it is the players who find those spaces. It's no longer acceptable for a number 10 to just stand in Zone 14 until someone finds them, for example (the same goes for any of those other spaces); it is about arriving in them, not waiting in them!

Press Resistance and Ball Retention

We briefly mentioned 'press resistance' above. This description applies to a player who is very difficult to dispossess, even when aggressively pressed. Body feints, quick feet, body movements, and 'hiding the ball' allow the best players to escape pressure. The likes of Moussa Dembele, Ryan Grabenberch, Pedri, and Luca Modric are examples of players who are outstanding at evading pressure. To have players who can, therefore, play in tight spaces and produce progressive or penetrative passes gives your team much greater attacking impetus.

Playing Under Pressure

One of the key aspects in gaining entry to those spaces relies on the ball getting there! Once it does, this space will not last for long, as defenders close it down. Often, these moments have a very 'now or never' feel. Playing under the pressure of time and the pressure of closing speed is a key feature of players who are most effective in these situations.

How often do you see a player line up a shot, for example, then take an extra touch, which leads to another one, and all the while, the window to take advantage of the opportunity is closing? The first split-second decision to delay means they miss the optimal moment to get the shot away, but no subsequent touch after that can undo the lost opportunity.

It is crucial, therefore, that fast, clinical, correct decisions are made in those tight spaces.

Conclusion

Gaining positional advantage is broad. It can happen with just the single orientation of a player's body to how the full team block is located on the pitch, to stop teams getting behind the defensive line easily or otherwise. It is static and dynamic. If you get into zone 14 or the wider channels in the box enough times, you will create goal-scoring chances. If you keep the opposition out of those areas, you should reduce the number of chances you concede.

Positional superiority (and its dynamic superiority counterpart) nicely rounds off the impact that all five superiorities have on the game of football. Although we have pulled them apart to study them more closely, we see that the more we do so, the more they influence each other.

TACTICAL TASK 35 – LIGHTBULB MOMENT

WHAT WAS YOUR GREATEST LIGHTBULB MOMENT FROM THIS CHAPTER?

HOW CAN YOU IMPROVE YOUR UNDERSTANDING OF THIS IDEA?

Cooperative Superiority
Our Players are Better Together Than Yours

Several years back, there was a stunning video of Lionel Messi and Dani Alves warming up before a game for Barcelona. On the hallowed turf at the Camp Nou, the diminutive South American pair passed the ball aerially to each other, using two touches, over a distance of approximately 30 metres. I am sure you'll have seen other high-level teammates doing something similar. If you have never seen it, get on *YouTube* and take a look.

This pair is the first that comes to my mind when telling the story of players 'cooperating' – not just in an indulgent pre-game routine, but on the pitch, too. They seemed to have a radar and a sixth sense about how the other would move and position themselves. Later, Messi had this with Jordi Alba, the opposite full-back in *that* Barcelona era.

> **TACTICAL TASK 36**
>
>
>
> NOTE DOWN ANY PLAYERS IN YOUR TEAM WHO YOU FEEL COOPERATE ESPECIALLY WELL TOGETHER. THIS WILL MOST LIKELY BE ON THE FIELD, BUT YOU CAN RECORD ANY OFF-FIELD SOCIAL TOGETHERNESS THAT THEY MAY HAVE, AS WELL. HOW CAN YOU FOSTER THESE CONNECTIONS MORE?

This cooperation does not just end with two mates who take to the field and dovetail well. From a tactical point of view, we can see this cooperation scale from a *two-player* connection to a *unit* to a whole team synergy – and even beyond into *whole squad* connections.

When talking about cooperation, we will often think about social connections, teamwork, leadership, followership, the motivational roles of team members, paintballing, raft-building and team barbeques. Whilst all those ideas can certainly influence a team's success, we will, however, hone in on the 'task' or tactical superiorities that can be built through these connections and on-field relationships.

Tactical Communication

Raymond Verheijen is a very divisive figure in football coaching circles whilst also one of the most thought-provoking. His area of speciality is a mix of sports science, tactical knowledge and common sense – often brutally told. Even during a quick scan of his work, you will find that controversy surrounds him – especially when it comes to his focus on the injury records of certain head coaches – and central to this criticism is not just fitness training for fitness' sake but football-fitness training for the sake of a better functioning team.

Playing Your Best Team

One of the cornerstones of Verheijen's work in senior professional environments is about keeping players fit and fresh so that a coach can play their "best team" together more often.

This idea, as basic as it might sound, is far from the traditional idea of simply putting 11 of the *qualitatively* best players you have on the field and then sitting back and watching the magic happen. It is more layered and complex than that. It uses team synergy to give your team a tactical advantage – "creating a surplus", as Shane Battier, *2014 NBA Teammate of the Year*, put it.

Here, we are not talking about your 11 best qualitative players – we are talking about relationships and communication, about understanding the habits and tendencies of your teammates, about having a group of players that all row in the same direction in all aspects of play. Partnerships, units, teams and squads that can be considered cooperatively superior to others will be characterised by this shared, tacit knowledge of group tactics and what to collectively do in certain situations.

TACTICAL TASK 37

CHOOSE WHAT YOU CONSIDER TO BE YOUR BEST QUALITATIVE XI. YOU MAY EVEN DO THIS USING A RANGE OF FORMATIONS.

REPEAT THE PROCESS. THIS TIME, HOWEVER, CHOOSE THE PLAYERS YOU FEEL HAVE THE BEST ATTITUDE, TEAM ETHIC, AND COOPERATION.

ONCE COMPLETE: HOW, IF AT ALL, DOES YOUR ANSWER ABOVE AFFECT THE FUTURE SELECTIONS

> **YOU MAY MAKE? ARE THE SAME 11 PLAYERS FLEXIBLE ENOUGH TO PLAY IN DIFFERENT SELECTIONS?**
>
> **DURING WHAT GAME STATES WOULD YOU CHOOSE YOUR QUALITATIVE BEST XI?**
>
> **DURING WHAT GAME STATES WOULD YOU CHOOSE YOUR COOPERATIVE BEST XI?**

Partnerships

You could probably reel off the best footballing partnerships you have seen in your lifetime. We have already spoken about Messi and his Barcelona comrades at the beginning of the chapter. Other partnerships that come to mind quite quickly are Vidic and Ferdinand at Manchester United, Robben and Robery (aka "Robbery") at Bayern Munich – and the double World Cup-winning Brazilian strike pair of Pelé and Garrincha, who never lost whilst playing together for their national team.

You could also offer some partnerships that have the reputation of not working, despite the *qualitative* level of their individual play. Steven Gerrard and Frank Lampard for the England National Team (although I believe that was a system flaw rather than a partnership one). Although not a 'pair', the Neymar, Messi, and Mbappe signings at PSG, made in real-life Football Manager-land, should have created a front three version of the USA Olympic Dream Team, but instead hit problems of compatibility, and in the team's balance of attacking and defending.[18] The trio (despite their immense qualitative capabilities) worked together to actually make their team performances, or certainly their expected results, poorer.

Compatibility is a brilliant word to describe the situation here. It challenges us to consider how playing relationships make our teams stronger or potentially weaker.

---

[18] Which is quite extraordinary considering how history sees the trio of Messi, Neymar, and Suarez at Barcelona. This may well nod to a superior team and club culture at Barcelona, rather than PSG!

There is huge power in knowing and being able to read the habits and intentions of your teammates, which is what we see when we talk about these successful partnerships. This compatibility could be something coached explicitly by coaches, or it may have developed implicitly between players. Either way, this process will, more often than not, take time to develop, and will also take playing time together to develop.

TACTICAL TASK 38

IDENTIFY THE MOST COMPATIBLE PARTNERSHIPS IN YOUR TEAM. HOW CAN YOU MAKE STRONG PARTNERSHIPS STRONGER? HOW CAN YOU MAKE THE WEAK PARTNERSHIPS STRONGER?

EXPLORE HOW THESE PARTNERSHIPS BECOME DISRUPTED WHEN YOU USE SUBSTITUTES OR ROTATE YOUR TEAM.

My take on the "playing your best team" point made by Verheijen is not exclusively about qualitative levels. Rather, he promotes the idea that the more players play together, the stronger these cooperative partnerships and connections grow. This, in turn, leads players to develop a more *intuitive* understanding of the game, habits, and skillsets of their teammates.

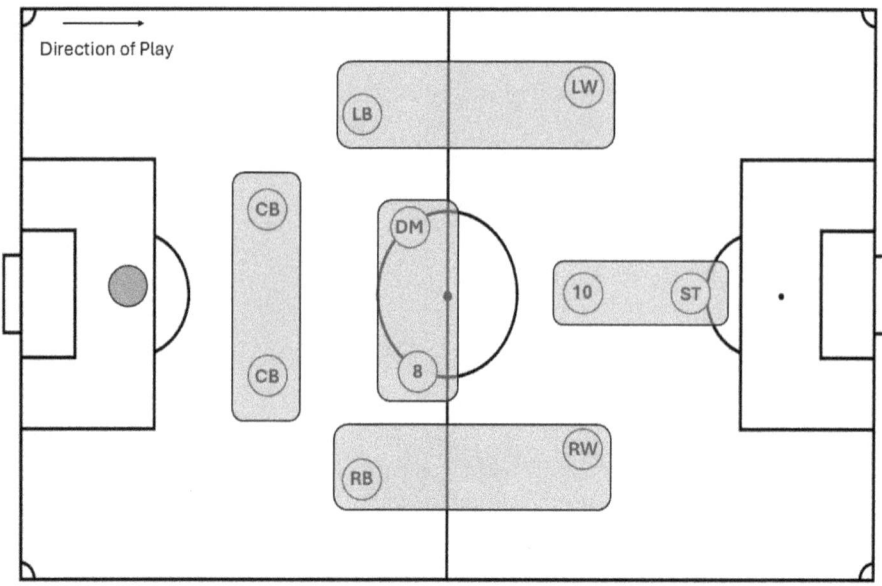

'Traditional' football partnerships within the team

The pitch above provides a simple example of common tactical partnerships that we think about when describing the game.

The intuitive (often described as 'telepathic') understanding between two players, however, does not necessarily need to involve direct partnerships like in the image above. Earlier in the chapter, I mentioned Messi (let's just call him a 'forward', which often depended on his role as either winger, false 9 or deeper playmaker) and Jordi Alba (left-back). Think about left-side centre-back Virgil van Dijk playing cross-field passes to right-winger Mo Salah, or the brilliant relationship between deep-lying midfielder Cesc Fabregas and striker Diego Costa whilst at Chelsea.

In an interview, Fabregas, now a coach himself – and always thoughtful in his analysis of the game – spoke about "knowing" that Costa would start running in behind the defence as soon as the midfielder had the ball, even in a small amount of time and space on the ball. Salah, adding a further layer to his connections and partnerships with teammates, would describe how his goalkeeper at Liverpool, Alisson Becker, would 'know' that the Egyptian would make a counter-attacking forward run, should the keeper catch the ball. Alisson has assisted Salah in scoring goals in the Premier League against Norwich City, Manchester United, Manchester City, and one (of sorts) against

Tottenham Hotspur, too. An indirect partnership that led to big outcomes against big opponents in big moments.

TACTICAL TASK 39

ARE THERE ANY NON-PARTNERSHIP RELATIONSHIPS IN YOUR TEAM? ARE THERE ANY YOU MAY WANT TO CULTIVATE MORE? HOW CAN YOU DEVELOP THIS PARTNERSHIP?

Units

We can also up the ante on tacit tactical relationship-building and cooperative superiorities by looking at famous *units* that make the sum of their parts stronger than their individual characteristics. Examples that quickly roll off the tongue would be the famous Back Four of AC Milan in the 1990s, the Champions League dominating midfield trio of Modric, Kross, and Casemiro at Real Madrid, or Busquets, Xavi, and Iniesta at Barcelona. Front threes of Tevez, Rooney, and Ronaldo at Manchester United, Messi, Suarez, and Neymar at Barcelona; Bale, Benzema, and Cristiano Ronaldo at Real Madrid also spring to mind; the list could go on and on.

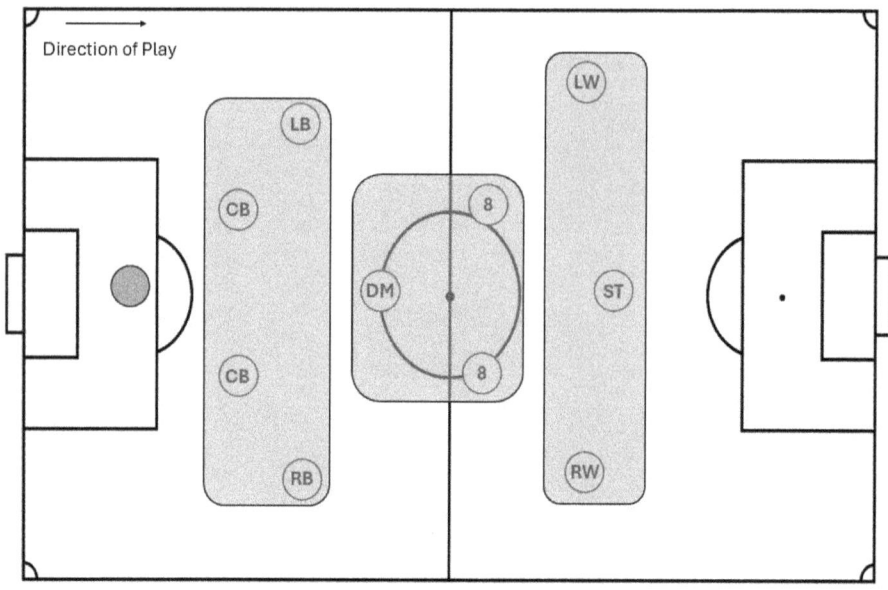

Traditional football units within the team

Again, as the image above presents, there are traditional units – back fours, midfield threes, front threes, etc. But again, we can – and *must* – expand our thinking from what a traditional 'unit' once meant and start to observe teams through cooperation that may actually reshape these units. Jose Mourinho famously would have defensive midfielder Claude Makelele warm up with the back four at Chelsea. Liverpool won Premier League and Champions League titles by utilising an "outside triangle" of Trent Alexander-Arnold, Jordan Henderson, and Mo Salah on Liverpool's right-hand side.

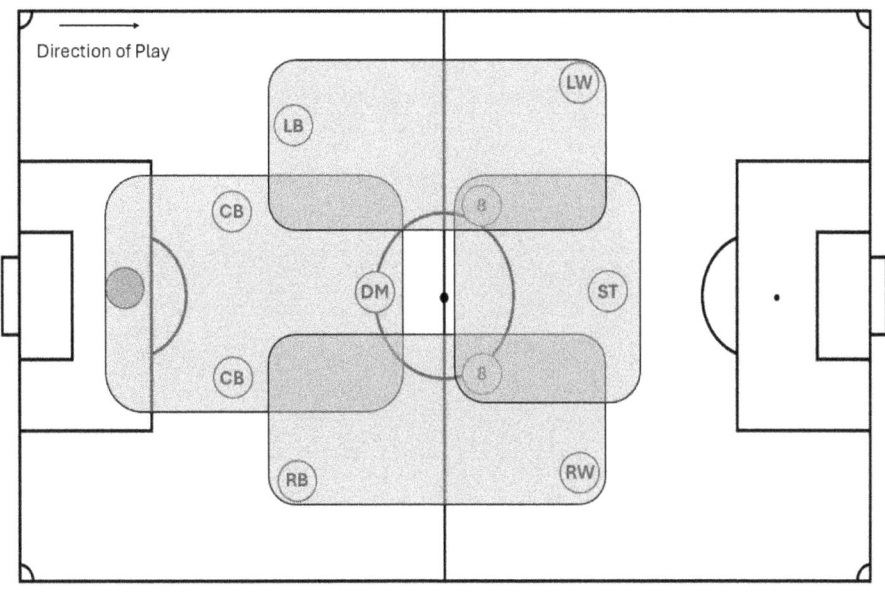

Expanding how we see 'units' of players in football

Interestingly, in the run-up to Euro 2016, two notable national team squads somewhat reshared and 're-grouped' their units, although neither seemed to make any major stir in the media. Now, whilst I believe these nuanced changes went more under the radar than they should have (certainly in mainstream punditry), I also believe it is a sign that football and football coaches are now evolving their thought processes around team/squad make-ups. Ahead of the tournament, Germany, carrying only one out-and-out striker, grouped all the attackers together on their squad list, whether a striker, number 10, attacking midfielder, wide forward, etc.

Even more dramatic and noteworthy were the ideas of the Italian National Team. Instead of the usual categories of Goalkeepers, Defenders, Midfielders and Forwards, they added a fifth distinct category – Wide Players. This category was not just wingers. It gathered what we would traditionally see as full-backs, wide midfielders, and wide attackers – and put them in the same bracket. So, players that would otherwise have been distributed between the three traditional units – for example, Mateo Darmian (defender), Antonio Candreva (midfield) and Federico Bernardeschi (forward) – were grouped together instead. A clear sign that the wide functions of the team would be made up by wide players with different characteristics in different moments.

TACTICAL TASK 40

UNIT ANALYSIS.

WHICH TRADITIONAL UNIT OF YOUR TEAM COOPERATES BEST/WORST? HOW CAN YOU AFFECT THIS?

WHICH 'NON-TRADITIONAL' UNITS CAN YOU DEVELOP AND OPTIMISE IN YOUR TEAM?

The Whole Team Function

In that particular Italian squad (mentioned above) was a player who is now a current head coach, Thiago Motta. In 2019, the Brazilian-born former midfielder famously hit the back page headlines with a 'new' formation – something he called a "2-7-2". Now, behind the mysterious, somewhat clickbait headline, Motta was essentially describing what most of us would see as a GK:4-3-3 (below). However, this refinement from Motta again shows just how modern coaches are starting to rethink how they see players and the team functioning together. The image below is taken directly from my book, *Coaching Youth Football*, which investigates deeper how coaches are rethinking the way they see players working together and their teams performing.

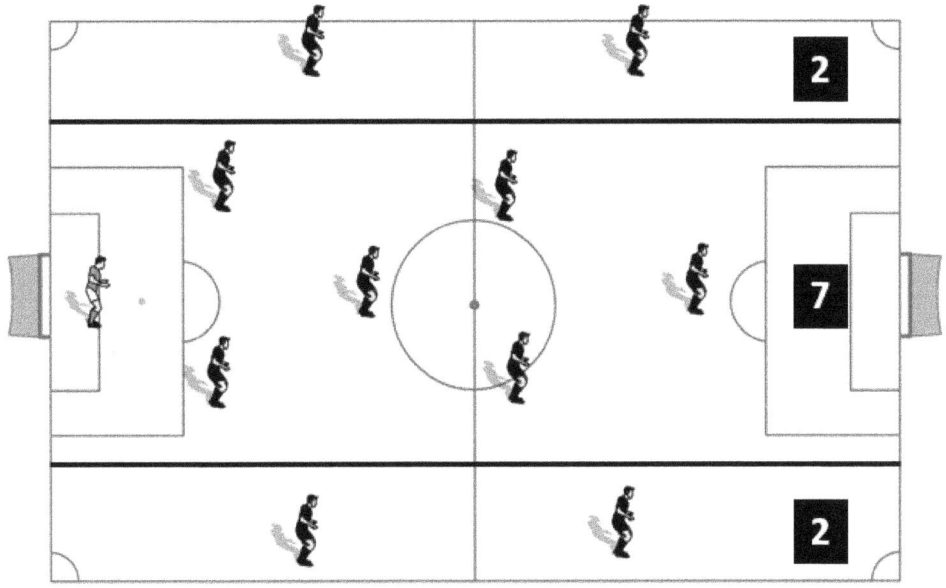

Thiago Motta's infamous 2-7-2 Formation

Instead of adding the goalkeeper as the '1' or "GK" every time we talk about GK:4-3-3 or 1:3-4-3, Motta includes the goalkeeper within a unit, although not necessarily one that you may expect – in the midfield one!

When considering how the whole team functions, we should consider ourselves very lucky to be able to freely access games, material, and ideas from the world's top coaches and clubs. The 'Game Model' of such coaches as Motta allow us to investigate and analyse, in real-time, the cooperative necessity needed to play the game successfully.

As a vehicle to explore whole-team cooperation, we can again utilise the *Four Moments of the Game* model – in possession, out of possession – and the transitional moments between both. There is a plethora of available information, for example, about how Guardiola's 'positional play' allows his teams to dominate possession in games. Then, further info about how this may differ from the positional play ideas of Roberto de Zerbi or Hansi Flick – or indeed how 'relationism' or direct or counter-attacking play contrasts entirely with it. We can analyse how Ranieri's Leicester City or Simeone's Atletico Madrid used effective transitions to win their respective leagues.

All successful team tactics involve high levels of cooperation as a necessity. The worst *teams* that we see, even if they do not have the worst players, are the teams whose make-up does not allow them to cooperatively function correctly. These teams, in particular, can be a major source of frustration and ridicule from the industry when teams do not synergise to the level their talent predicts they should. Examples may include the tournament performances of the England national team for several decades or Manchester United under a series of head coaches since the departure of Sir Alex Ferguson.[19]

TACTICAL TASK 41

WHICH COACH OR COACHES CAN YOU USE AS YOUR 'GAME MODEL ROLE MODEL'? IN OTHER WORDS, THOSE YOU CAN RESEARCH AND USE TO INSPIRE YOU AND YOUR WAY OF PLAYING.

Team Cooperation – Out of Possession

To deeply explore team cooperation, however, we will zoom in on the out-of-possession or defending principles of the game.

The most important principle when we talk about defending is *Team Compactness* – and it is also a very clear way of demonstrating effective team cooperation. A team that is compact is one that is very difficult to play through, around, or over.[20]

I like to think of a compact team as being like a fist that is powerful when you punch, versus an uncompact team that is like an open palm and which – therefore – does not function with the same power. All players in all positions in every team will have defensive responsibilities, although some will clearly have more than others depending on the team, the individuals within the

---

[19] Somewhat ironically, the team that won Ferguson's final Premier League with United was arguably a much poorer qualitative team that any that has followed it!

[20] It is possible that football can be summarised by two teams trying to play through, around, or over the other's defensive block to create chances to score goals.

team, the game model, or other circumstances. If you cooperate well on a team level, all 11 players will take an active part (or their *specific* active part – more on that later) in team defending.

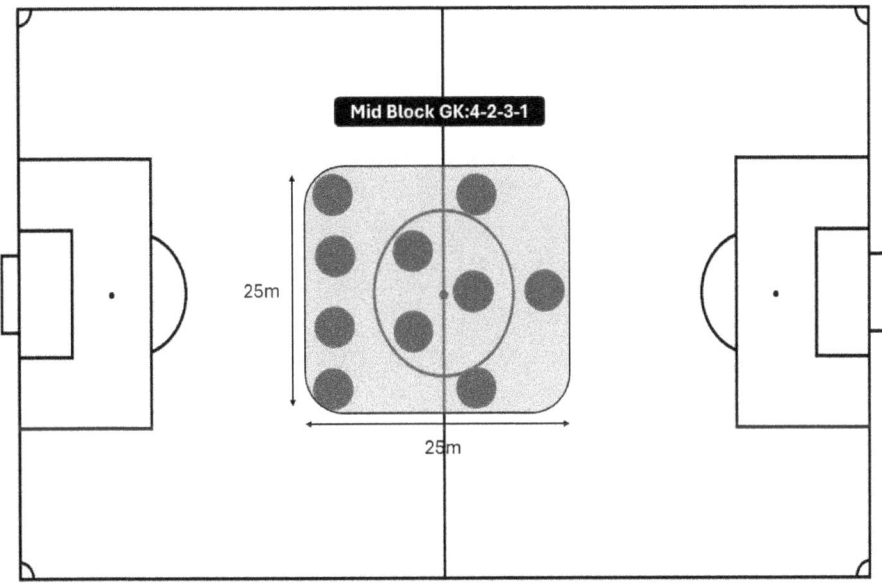

A Compact GK:4-2-3-1 'Mid-Block'

We often use the term 'block' when discussing team compactness, the ultimate form of team cooperation when out of possession. A compact block is essentially the connected positioning of the ten outfield players to stop the opponent from progressing forward. The distances and connections within this block are very important. I have spent a number of years working abroad with players whose first language is not English. This requires me to be very straightforward and concise in my language. So, when discussing team defending, we have learned to use the word 'compact' and the word 'connect'. If I ask a player to 'connect', this means that they must take up a position where they 'attach' to their nearest teammates that join them to the block. The distances involved in the connection are difficult to measure mathematically, but a useful rule of thumb is whether players are close enough together to not be played *through* easily, but far enough apart so they are not easily played *around*.

Now, the overall size of this block is of extreme importance. If all ten outfield players, for example, were in a 10 x 10 metre compact square, they would be *too compact* and would be played *around and over* without too much discomfort for the opposition. Likewise, if they were too spread out (like an open palm), the opposition could play *through* them more easily. Conventional wisdom (and this refers to elite, adult, professional players) is that a compact team will cover the pitch horizontally and vertically using a 25-metre squared distance. This 25-metre 'vertical' distance between the back line and the front player was popularised by revolutionary Italian coach Arrigo Sacchi, a man who was renowned for his work around pressing.[21] For youth or grassroots teams, this block size may be too small and prevent them from physically being able to cover the pitch efficiently. For example, if you look at the diagram above again, expecting a 12-year-old to cover the same distance from being 'compact' to the touchline to press a winger repeatedly, in the same way a senior professional player would, is inadvisable.

So, whilst making this 25 x 25 metre mathematical reference point is useful, what is more useful is asking the question in the task below:

TACTICAL TASK 42

WHAT DOES MY TEAM LOOK LIKE WHEN THEY ARE DEFENSIVELY COMPACT? IS IT A SOLID BLOCK OR CAN IT BE EASILY PLAYED THROUGH OR AROUND (OR OVER)?

Compact blocks come in three broad forms – the 'mid-block' as above, and bookending it – the 'high block' and 'low block' as per the image below. (You could, theoretically, get into further subtlety by having a 'mid-high block' or 'low-mid block', etc.)

---

[21] Sacchi is to pressing football history what Cruyff is to possession football. A coach who has had huge influence over how modern defending and pressing looks.

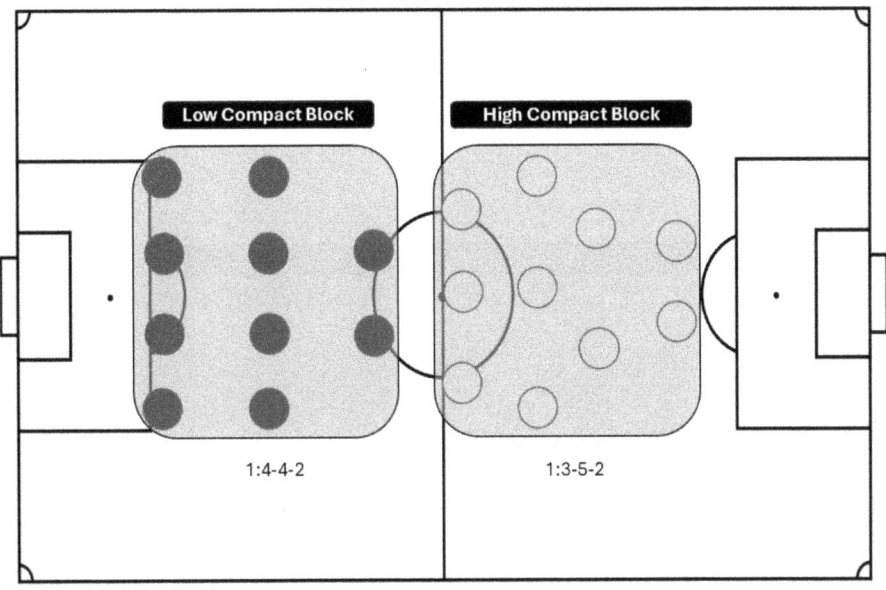

Two compact blocks: one in a 'low' GK:4-4-2 and one in a 'high' GK:3-5-2

You may have noticed that in all three depictions of compact blocks (in both the images above), I have intentionally used different formations. This was very strategic on my part to reinforce that all routine base formations can be organised compactly (I use the word 'routine' to refer essentially to the ten formations set out by Marcelo Bielsa in the opening chapter) and not 'special' formations that may be used in emergency 'Game State' cases – e.g., throwing defensive caution to the wind for the last five minutes of a game when you need to score!

Base formations can, however, also morph into separate structures depending on the height of the block, as per the image below, or indeed the amount of time spent in the block.[22] This can be something quite seamless, like the below example where the two wide attackers drop effortlessly into the midfield line, but it may be really pronounced with teams that have two (or more!) completely different structures when defending in a high block compared to defending in a low block. Either way, where you are functioning defensively as a team in one compact shape, or morphing in and out of other

---

[22] For example, a back 3 formation may defend situationally as a back 4 in a mid or low block, particularly if the ball is in a wide area, but will eventually fall into a back 5 the longer the team is defending the goal and the box.

shapes in certain situations, how players relate and cooperate together is of essential importance.

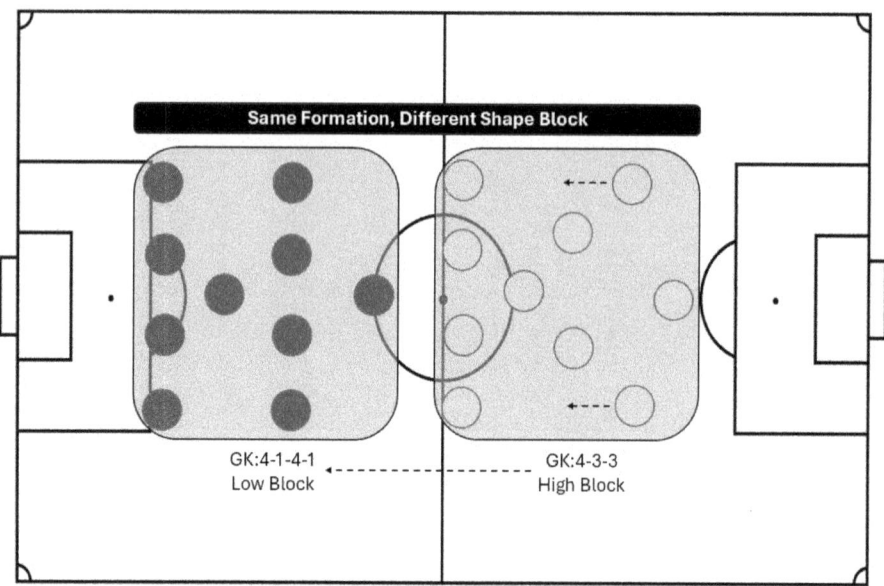

A GK:4-3-3 team defending in two different shapes, depending on the location of the block

Ultimately, the shape of the team when defending in different moments is important here, but the critical part is that team members understand and can cooperate effectively to seamlessly defend as a group with one intention. In the same way, a possession-based phase would see players cooperating to carry out on-ball actions. For example, in teams that use heavy build-up tactics, you would see teammates moving to support the ball carrier playing a short pass.

A whole team functioning tactically together is considered the holy grail of tactical football coaching. And this functioning is often incorrectly seen as all 11 players having their 'fair share' of attacking and defensive work, for example.

A little earlier, I mentioned players *sharing* defensive duties. It is commonly accepted that all players have both attacking and defensive duties – we often hear that the striker is considered the team's first defender, and the goalkeeper and centre-backs are the team's first attackers. So, there is already an acknowledgement that different players have a different balance of attacking and defending. Indeed, an old scouting document from Tottenham Hotspur (which I am sure now is no longer in use by the club) actually gave percentage ratios of attacking/defensive responsibilities by position:

> *Full-back: 75% defender*
>
> *Centre-half: 80% defender*
>
> *'Controller' (deep-lying midfielder): 50% defender*
>
> *Number 8: 50% defender*
>
> *Number 10: 30% defender; 70% attacker*
>
> *Forward ('number 9): 20% defender; 80% attacker*
>
> *Wide forwards (numbers 7 & 11): 25% defender; 75% attacker*

Tottenham Hotspur Defending: Attacking Positional Ratios

TACTICAL TASK 43

CREATE YOUR OWN VERSION OF TOTTENHAM'S *DEFENDING: ATTACKING POSITIONAL RATIOS*.

WRITE DOWN THE PLAYERS AND THEIR POSITIONS IN YOUR SQUAD. (IF A PLAYER PLAYS MULTIPLE POSITIONS, WRITE THEIR NAME DOWN AGAINST EVERY POSITION THEY MAY PLAY). LIKE AT TOTTENHAM, CAN YOU ATTRIBUTE A PERCENTAGE ATTACKING/DEFENDING RATIO TO EACH ONE, DEPENDING ON THEIR POSITION.

When I first started coaching, everything was fair and mirrored. I asked the same defensively of both wingers, for example. Both full-backs had the same balance of attacking and defending, etc. It is possible, however, to create highly functioning teams where these defensive roles and responsibilities are not shared equally at all. Mo Salah defended less (and later) than Sadio Mané. Gareth Bale more than Cristiano Ronaldo.

We see countless examples where certain players, who are saved physically and mentally for their ability in-possession, are released from defensive duties. Even a coach like Jose Mourinho, famed for his focus on defensive work, would release special attacking players like Eden Hazard and Cristiano Ronaldo from defensive duties to allow them to affect the game more at the other end. We see this commonly with midfielders (maybe the central idea of midfielders contributing to both attack and defensive allows this to prevail); some have roles that require more defensive or attacking responsibilities than their compatriots in the centre of the pitch. Like the Salah and Ronaldo examples above, this can refer to other positions, too. You may have one fullback who joins attacks more regularly than the other, or one centre-back who may drive forwards in possession or play more forward passes than the other.

It is essential to create a cooperating team where players know and understand their defensive and offensive duties, the duties of others, and *why* these duties may differ. Understanding is the essence of cooperation.

Substitutes and Using Your Squad

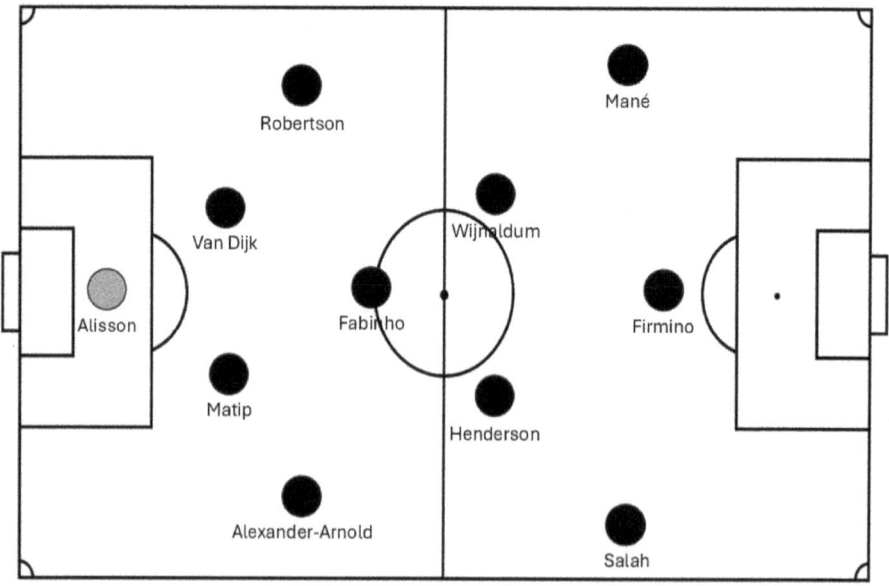

Famous Liverpool XI under Jürgen Klopp

I am sure most of you will immediately recognise the above team as arguably being the strongest and most frequently used XI of Liverpool FC under Jürgen Klopp. The team that won the Premier League in 2020 and Champions League in 2019. Right? Wrong.

Because of injuries, suspensions, one-off selection decisions, etc, this famed XI only started together once (in the 2019 Champions League Final itself, no less)! Furthermore, they never ever played a full 90-minute competitive football match together!

So, along with being a really good piece of trivia for quiz night, there is a clear learning outcome for all coaches at all levels: your entire squad and your matchday substitutes are a vital part of the cooperative level of your team. To win all before them, this "best XI" unequivocally needed the input of those in and around the wider squad too – and they needed them game-in, game-out.

So, now we have a potential contradiction – do we play with our "best team", or do we need to think beneath the surface of what this actually means? Even at the professional level, it is impossible to compete with only 11 players who play every week, even if we adhere to Verheijen's ideas around playing with your best team. Many factors will prevent this from happening, as discussed above.

In youth development football teams, it is openly accepted that playing time should be shared between players, depending on your philosophy, your team's philosophy, or your club's philosophy. So, whilst professional or senior-level competitive teams should not make equal playing time a requirement (like with the kids), the concept and benefits of all players playing regularly within your team to build cooperative strength and habits is crucial.

Along with considerations of winning and losing, there is a social, psychological and humanistic view to all this, too. If you are running a football team, then having a camp of players who feel involved and important is huge. So, that player who is *always* a substitute needs a share of attention and game time. You will 'need' him or her at some point in a game, in a season, or in a tournament. You often hear of players being 'brought in from the cold' because a coach suddenly needs them to play because of some crisis or other. Even if this player is the weakest 'qualitative' link in your squad, they have got to be used – in some capacity – in the regular cycle of games to keep them mentally stimulated and to develop playing relationships and a cooperative understanding with the group.

This piece of the puzzle is sadly missing from the coaching equation that is normally discussed in coaching circles. One coach and author aiming to change this is Sammy Landers, the world's first "substitution coach" and author of *Finishers – How to Create Your Own Super Sub*. Despite the increasing role of substitutes as the game has evolved through the decades, and growing squad sizes in the professional game, Lander remains convinced that no player likes being a substitute, and is something that needs to be carefully managed.

He describes the need for giving substitutes a process to work through – both in training and on matchday. The traditional procedures for substitutes and squad players during the training week is largely to prepare the first XI for the upcoming game, and then on game day, it usually involves them being involved in an after-thought of activities before, during, and at half-time in the game. Then, depending on the minutes played, they will conduct a set of pitch sprints or "top-up runs", designed to replicate some high-intensity physical output that they missed out on during the game. When you consider that matchday is the most special day of the week for everyone – players especially – this is quite the anti-climax!

Lander advocates that those who may 'finish' the game, rather than start, are provided with a process that is valuable. This includes training sessions that prepare them for 'what-if' moments that may happen on game day. If a defensive midfielder is brought on with 10 minutes to go, what will their function most likely be, and what will be the likely game-state? If a centre-back is replaced, maybe this will be for something extreme – like injury or serious underperformance. If an attacker is brought on, this could be to chase a goal or add some energy to counter-attacks if the team is protecting a lead. If an attacking midfielder replaces a defensive one, then the team will likely be chasing the game.

These are general examples, but you will have extra context for this in your environment – "We are bottom of the league, and on Saturday we are playing against the top team. Most likely, we will be losing or trying to remain competitive as the game advances. In this potential game, what will the requirements be for those players who will come in and finish the game?" US soccer coach Jill Ellis famously renamed her substitutes "game-changers" in an attempt to keep them mentally involved and highlight the importance and potential impact of these players on the game.

In *Soccermatics*, author and mathematician David Sumpter identifies the optimal moments during a match to make substitutions (back when teams were limited to three changes per game). He recommends the 58th, 73rd, and 79th minutes as the ideal times to make changes, based on mathematical models designed to enhance the impact of fresh players. Additionally, Sumpter suggests that when a team is trailing, introducing a more offensive player as early as the 32nd minute can be advantageous. Conversely, when holding a lead, substituting in a more defensive player around the 47th minute can help secure the advantage. These strategies are tailored to maximise a team's chances, depending on the game's dynamics.

Whilst it is common and obvious to think that Player A is qualitatively better than Player B, and – therefore – A will play all the time, this can actually fluctuate. Of course, over time, players can improve and regress, lose form, gain form, have a hot streak, etc., but one of the ways that this fluctuates in-game is through fatigue. Sumpter calculated that although Player A is considered better, after periods of intense playing time, the fatigue-less Player B may now be more effective and therefore 'better' from that moment. Therefore, to use Verheijen's words, playing your "best team" will, every game, be more than just 11 players.

As a coach, your behaviour is speaking to everyone all the time. Involving all players at your disposal is therefore important for many reasons – from using their skillset to win a game, or keeping them stimulated when not playing as much as they want to. Ole Gunnar Solskjaer never wanted to be a substitute for Manchester United but tells a brilliant story about Ferguson increasing his confidence, even during a game he never played. A simple comment from the coach at half-time suggested that if Manchester United had not scored by the 75th minute, the Norwegian striker would be substituted in, and he would get the goal they needed. He said it in an utterly matter-of-fact way that the striker, speaking at the *Oslo Business Forum*, attributed that comment as being a key reason behind his dramatic late winning goal in the 1999 Champions League Final.

TACTICAL TASK 44

CREATE A NEW PROCESS THAT YOU CAN USE TO MANAGE AND MOTIVATE YOUR SQUAD PLAYERS AND SUBSTITUTES.

AT THE START OF THE SEASON, ATTRIBUTE HOW MUCH GAME TIME YOU WILL GIVE TO YOUR SQUAD PLAYERS. TO HELP YOU DO THIS, YOU CAN IMAGINE A CONVERSATION BETWEEN ARTETA AND A SQUAD PLAYER AT ARSENAL (IN 2024/25) – LET'S USE FULL-BACK TAKEHIRO TOMIYASU AS AN EXAMPLE. HE WON'T PLAY MUCH, AND HE WON'T EXPECT TO BE SELECTED IN THE FIRST XI MUCH, BUT THERE WILL NO DOUBT BE CRITICAL MOMENTS THROUGHOUT THE SEASON WHEN HE WILL BE NEEDED TO PLAY – AND MAYBE EVEN IN AN EMERGENCY, WHICH HE HAS DONE NUMEROUS TIMES FOR ARSENAL BEFORE. HE WILL ALSO KNOW FULL WELL THAT, IN THESE MOMENTS, HE WILL BE TASKED TO PLAY, FOR EXAMPLE, LEFT-BACK FOR A GAME OR TWO WHILE PLAYERS A AND B ARE UNAVAILABLE, BEFORE LOSING HIS PLACE ONCE EITHER ARE AVAILABLE AGAIN. NOT EXACTLY A SITUATION THAT MAY STIMULATE YOUR EGO (DESPITE WHAT WE THINK ABOUT THEIR SALARIES). YOU WANT THE BEST AND MOST PREPARED TOMIYASU YOU CAN HAVE.

INSTEAD OF THE SEASON ARRIVING AND TOMIYASU IS SIMPLY NOT SELECTED WEEK AFTER WEEK, HAVE A DIFFERENT CONVERSATION TO KEEP HIM MOTIVATED AND WITH AN

> EXPECTATION THAT YOU WILL BOTH AGREE ON.
>
> THE CONVERSATION MIGHT START WITH A QUESTION: "IF, BY THE END OF THE SEASON, WE COUNT HOW MANY GAMES YOU PLAY ACROSS ALL COMPETITIONS, HOW MANY WOULD YOU BE SATISFIED WITH?" NOW, THAT NUMBER MAY CHANGE FROM PLAYER TO PLAYER (THERE ARE SOME WHO, IN TOMIYASU'S POSITION, WOULD STILL SAY "ALL OF THEM"! IF THIS IS THE CASE, YOU MAY NEED TO TAKE CONTROL OF THE CONVERSATION AND TELL THEM INSTEAD: "I THINK A PRODUCTIVE SEASON FOR YOU WOULD BE TO PLAY IN 15-20 GAMES ACROSS ALL COMPETITIONS".
>
> IDEALLY, WHAT YOU WANT IS A CONSENSUS BETWEEN BOTH OF YOU, BUT ONE THAT IS EASILY ACHIEVABLE. THE CONVERSATION MAY GIVE YOU A MORE CONTENT SQUAD PLAYER AS THEY ARE IN THE KNOW ABOUT WHAT IS HAPPENING, BUT IT ALSO HOLDS YOU ACCOUNTABLE FOR THEIR GAME TIME.
>
> OBVIOUSLY, THINGS LIKE AVAILABILITY, INJURY, DISCIPLINE AND OTHER OUTSIDE FACTORS WILL AFFECT THIS. THIS SHOULD BE OPENLY EXPLAINED TO THE PLAYER, TOO.

Conclusion – Dynamic Cooperative Superiority

Whilst we have not explicitly spoken about dynamic superiority within a cooperative context, I certainly hope that this dynamism is implied:

Playing partnerships will not only be with traditional partners or traditional units (e.g., Fabregas and Costa, or Liverpool's wide triangle) but also

Cooperation changes depend on your team selection. Some players who are qualitatively poorer than others may offer more cooperation and, therefore, help their unit and team function to a higher level.

Cooperation extends beyond the first XI and into the squad players and substitutes. Your concept of having your "best team" may need challenging.

TACTICAL TASK 45 – LIGHTBULB MOMENT

WHAT WAS YOUR GREATEST LIGHTBULB MOMENT FROM THIS CHAPTER?

HOW CAN YOU IMPROVE YOUR UNDERSTANDING OF THIS IDEA?

Being Better
Other Superiorities

Right at the beginning of this journey through superiorities, we looked at the idea of being better. Ultimately, the final answer to any question about players or teams being 'better' can have multiple and multi-layered answers.

I think Vinicius Jnr. is a better football player than Rodri, but if I need a player to control a game, I will choose the Spaniard. If I want a player to make a difference in and around the box, I choose the Brazilian. If I need a makeshift centre-back, and I have Vini and Rodri on the bench to choose from, I will select Rodri. If I have a player running 1v1 towards the goalkeeper, I will select Vini.

Barcelona are a good team until you ask them to sit in a low block for 90 minutes. I would choose Atletico Madrid's team if I wanted to do that and get a result. Better is subjective (someone will probably disagree with my choices above), but it can also be circumstantial and malleable.

Dynamic Superiority

Among the myriad and mix of concepts that dictate success on the pitch, dynamic superiority stands as one of the most crucial yet not fully understood elements. Throughout this book, I have absorbed and interwoven the concept into the other superiorities rather than giving it a chapter of its own – such is the importance of dynamic superiority rather than its lack of importance. Not having a full chapter all to itself signifies its utility across all the other superiorities and an inability to talk about the rest of the game without including the dynamic-ness of the game of football.

Throughout the book, certain words have dominated the pages and should sit firmly at the front of your mind: *Movement. Fluid. Variable. Moments.* Etc. These are all words and concepts that sit under the 'Dynamic' headline. It is, therefore, worth taking a moment to look at dynamic superiority in isolation.

For absolute clarity, dynamic superiority is the ability of a player, a combination of players, or the team in full to create (and exploit) advantageous situations during certain moments of the game. Its central features are focused on movement, adaptability, and in-game intelligence to outmanoeuvre opponents.

The sheer enormity of the movements and collaborations possible in a football game means that one can never completely list all the possible ways that players can, essentially, move to advantage. Any list would become outdated very quickly.

For example, in an interview with *The Overlap*, former Leicester City goalkeeper Kasper Schmeichel spoke of his coach at Belgian side Anderlecht asking him to line up, in certain moments, at the right of a back three when the team was in possession. During the early stages of the team's build-up, it was his brief to move into this position with the idea of hitting long, diagonal passes to the team's left wing.

Of course, the timing of this movement to leave his position with the intention of receiving the ball (not just by leaving the sanctuary of the goal but by leaving the central area altogether) requires movement and a read of what is happening dynamically in those situations. The risk of a goalkeeper doing this must balance against the reward of doing it. While the goalkeeper needs some time and space to execute the long pass, he will also attract pressure due to the potential reward of the opponent regaining the ball and threatening the goal themselves.

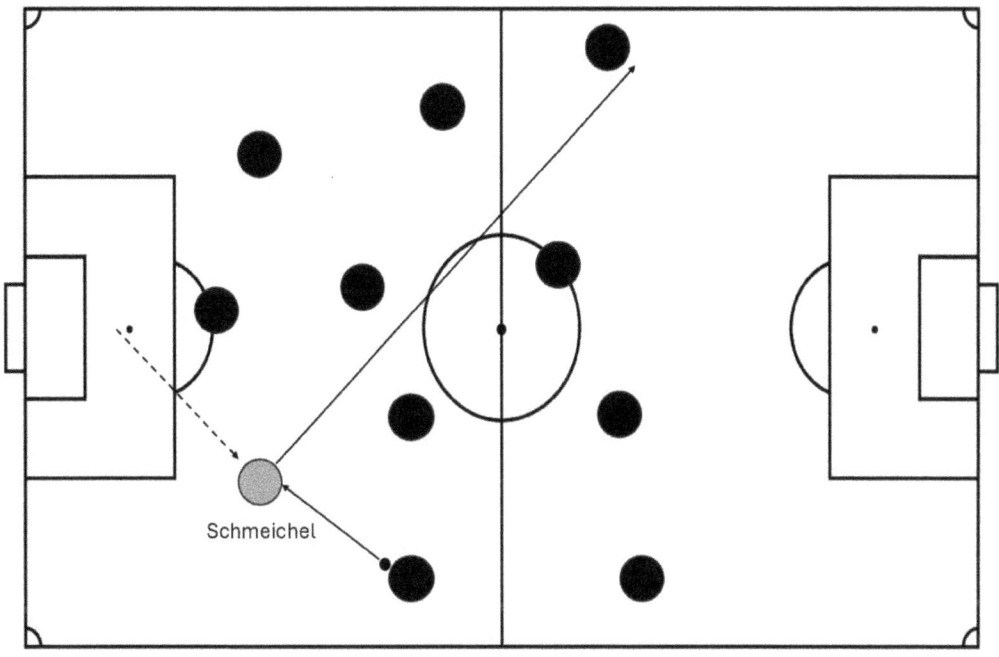

Visual representation of goalkeeper Kasper Schmeichel's role in moving into a position on the right side of a back three to hit diagonal passes to the left wing.

TACTICAL TASK 46

CONSIDERING THE ABOVE IDEA FROM SCHMEICHEL, HOW CAN YOU USE YOUR GOALKEEPER TO CREATE SUPERIORITY IN YOUR GAME?

In this interview with Schmeichel, former Manchester United full-back and former Valencia and England coach Gary Neville was on the panel. More known today for his punditry and TV analysis rather than his coaching, Neville was an early observer of the importance of dynamic movements from players in the modern game. Neville, and his colleague Jamie Carragher on English TV station Sky Sports, have a commendable trait of embracing the new and revolutionary ideas they witness, even when they break from the ideas of "their day" – which is not-so-common with former players in these positions.

A decade before Schmeichel's interview, when analysing attacker Philippe Coutinho, Neville spoke about modern players "moving into space instead of standing in space". Dynamic rather than static. During his playing career, Neville would have spent week after week playing with and against dangerous players who may have prioritised more stationary positioning over dynamic ones. Had Coutinho played in Neville's Manchester United team in the late 1990s or early 2000s, for example, there is little doubt that he would have played as a more static, traditional number 10, taking up a relatively fixed position between the opposition's defensive and midfield lines.

In the more modern game, however, players like the Brazilian Coutinho, who may have been profiled as pure number 10s in the past, are now required to play away from the congested central 'Zone 14' space that they once dominated. This has led them to become more flexible by starting games in other positions (mainly due to opposition teams clogging up the space in front of the defence with midfield players). Coutinho, for example, played a lot from the left, whilst having the ability and freedom to move into positions centrally or on the right.

In many ways, this period of change bred a form of attacker or attacking midfielder who could and should be able to play anywhere across the pitch in attacking zones, rather than get pigeon-holed as '10s' or 'wingers'. The likes of Coutinho, David Silva, Kevin de Bruyne, Luca Modric and many others, also played centrally as number 8s (and even deeper-lying midfield players in the case of the Croat). Some other traditional 10s play as strikers or wide forwards, such as Firmino, Mbappé or Jamal Musiala.

The skill now, however, is to *arrive* in those spaces between the lines, rather than wait there like an old-fashioned number 10. Coutinho would not stand and wait between the lines for his teammates to find him with the ball; he would move into these spaces to arrive there when the ball arrives or is free to arrive, much like Manchester United's Bruno Fernandes or Chelsea's Cole Palmer. The spaces themselves are also far more dynamic and moveable than before. As defenders and defensive midfielders tussle to shut critical spaces down from being exploited by attackers, other vacant spaces pop up situationally as a result – and often in the dangerous areas of the field that defensive formations just can't cover all at once. Many coaches will even call these players 'space-finders'; their job is to locate, arrive in, and exploit fluid spaces left by defences.

Developing players that can thrive in these dynamic environments is, therefore, a crucial responsibility of football coaches. On the training ground, static exercises with overly prescribed movements for players may well start to work against a game that is becoming even more fluid and flexible.

Dynamic superiority, therefore, is the continuous and thoughtful use of movement to create other superiorities – numerical, positional, qualitative or cooperative advantages. It thrives in moments of attacking play, transition, quick passing sequences, off-the-ball movement, and tactical fluidity. Both the examples above of Schmeichel and Coutinho contain ideas established in all other superiorities, too:

- Overloading key areas of the pitch to outnumber the opponent (numerical).
- Occupying optimal spaces to facilitate ball progression (positional).
- Exploiting individual skill mismatches to gain an edge in duels (qualitative).
- Working together with teammates in terms of mental ideas and physical movement to maximise these opportunities (cooperative).

From Individual to Group Dynamism

Dynamic superiority is the guiding principle in many team tactical systems, particularly those that prioritise fluidity and constant, consistent movement. Certain strategies leverage this concept to enhance a team's advantages and effectiveness, especially, but not exclusively, during the in-possession phases of their game.

Positional Play and Relationism
One of the primary methods many teams use to achieve dynamic superiority is known as 'Positional Play', a philosophy attributed to Dutch coaches Rinus Michels and Johan Cruyff, and further refined and modernised by Pep Guardiola. This approach involves strict positional rules to create numerical advantages in specific areas at certain times. This is done through structured,

organised movement, using third-man runs and movements to break defensive lines and, ultimately, enter high-probability goal-scoring areas.

The dynamic movement involved requires some players to rotate and swap positions in an attempt to destroy the opposition's defensive and marking tactics. The positioning rarely changes, just the players who occupy them. So, if the wide winger comes inside into the half-space, for example, the local full-back or local midfielder will then become the 'wide' player, even if only temporarily.

Along with this movement and rotation, Positional Play teams must want expert players to remain in their expert positions. Whilst Kevin de Bruyne receiving the ball in the widest channel is not a bad thing, it is so much better if he can receive it in the half-space to pass, cross, and hurt the opponent. Similarly, you would prefer speedster Jérémy Doku receiving in wide areas, Haaland arriving in goal-scoring positions, and Rodri backing up the play from central areas. Rotations, therefore, need to be carefully presented to ensure that expert players are affecting the game in expert ways – to maximise potential qualitative superiorities.

Up until the 24/25 season, I have watched Guardiola's Manchester City line up predominantly in a GK:4-3-3 base formation, and I would estimate that this happens about 80% of the time. During the other 20%, I saw him use formations with a back three, a front two, a midfield four, etc. Irrespective, Guardiola's teams always end up – when the ball is in the final third – set-up in some variation of GK:2-3-5 (or GK:0-2-3-5, as we will touch on below).

You will also see Guardiola's teams line up with different *types* of players being squad-rotated in the same positions. For example, he will have a rampaging attacking full-back at left-back one week, then a midfielder at left-back to 'invert' the next week. In week three, both full-backs will be centre-backs by trade. Position dynamism at its best!

> **TACTICAL TASK 47**
>
>
>
> **THE NEXT TIME YOU GET A CHANCE TO WATCH MANCHESTER CITY, EVEN ON YOUTUBE, TRY TO DO SO FROM A 'TACTICAL CAMERA' AND OBSERVE HOW THE TEAM DYNAMICALLY SHAPE-SHIFTS FROM ANY OF THE ABOVE INTO A GK:2-3-5, MOST OF THE TIME.**

Pitched as the opposite[23] of Positional Play is the less-known but growing philosophy of play of *Relationism* in football. This is a tactical approach that emphasises fluid interactions and player relationships instead of the often rigid positional structures of Positional Play.

Relationism thrives on the spontaneity of player movement, the connectivity between multiple players often occupying the same area of the field, and mutual, cooperative understanding between players. It would not be uncommon in relationist teams, for example, for both wingers to occupy the same channel or pocket of space… something barely conceivable within Positional Play. Once together, the objective of the players is to then combine to hurt the defence in that area, or attract defensive pressure and exploit the opponent elsewhere, much like the 'overload to isolate' concept we spoke about earlier.

Instead of instructing players on where exactly to be, relationism encourages them to instinctively or intuitively 'feel' how to move based on BOTS – the ball's location, the position of the opponents, their teammates' positions, the spaces involved – and the unfolding dynamics of the game before them. It relies on cooperation – trust, improvisation, and synergy – often forming what can feel like (and *is!*) organised chaos to opposition and observers.

---

[23] Both philosophies are not 'opposite', they are just different in their main ideas. Both are based on attacking, dominating attacks, regaining the ball quickly, etc., but both have different central aims for doing so.

Brazilian coach Fernando Diniz is widely regarded as the most high-profile modern proponent of relationist football. His Fluminense team, particularly during the 2022–2023 period, became the poster child of relationism in action and ironically faced off against Guardiola's Manchester City in the *Club World Cup Final* in December 2023.

The team's unpredictability of movement made them difficult to prepare for, as opponents struggled to anticipate player movements or deal with them with traditional defensive schemes. If even the players did not have a script about where they might move and when, how on earth was the opposition supposed to!?

Although they would lose heavily to Manchester City, Fluminense's application of relationism under Diniz reached its peak that same year as they won the Copa Libertadores earlier in 2023 (which qualified them for the Club World Cup), playing what many fans and pundits described as some of the most beautiful football in South America. Players coached by Diniz during this period often credited him not just for the tactical system but for giving them confidence, freedom, and joy in playing – all outcomes that coaches of young players would strive for, let alone elite, professional continental champions.

Defending & Transitions

It is easy to look at movement and dynamism as being exclusively an in-possession aspect. However, fluidity, movement, and dynamism – when defending and in transition – can be used to produce advantages, too.

A team, for example, may defend with two, three, four, or five players in their defensive line, depending on the *situation* of the game. Just because a team may line up with four defenders does not mean they will always defend with a back-line of four. In other rest-defence moments (where a team in possession organises itself to defend should they lose the ball), some dominant teams will play with both centre-backs well into the opponent's half, meaning, effectively, a back line of zero (hence the GK:*0-2-3-5* reference above). This is so they can defend in the opponent's half, press high, and counter-press when they lose the ball, and thus defend higher.

The technique of pressing, for example, whether as an individual or as a team, is a crucial element of dynamic superiority. Individually, players fundamentally learn from early in their development to 'move as the ball moves', slowing down as they reach the target of their press. Collectively, teams that excel in high pressing can create temporary or situational numerical superiority by aggressively closing down spaces, blocking passing lanes, and forcing turnovers in dangerous areas. All of which are extremely dynamic skills that require decision-making and physical mobility.

As noted earlier in the book, players no longer just defend 1v1 against singular opponents. Out-of-possession players often have 'hybrid' marking roles where they will press various different opponents, depending on BOTS and whatever situational responses are necessary in a given situation. Some players in some teams that utilise hybrid pressing and dynamic defensive structures may be tasked with positioning themselves to press or take direct responsibility for the pressure of three to four different players, depending on what happens next with the ball.

Transitions

Fast transitions, both in attack and defence, are vital to achieving overall dynamic superiority. Teams like Real Madrid under Carlo Ancelotti or Zinedine Zidane have showcased excellence in transition play, using pace and directness to exploit defensive vulnerabilities.

In attacking transitions, teams use verticality to rapidly move the ball upfield (quick forward passes, runs with the ball, or runs without the ball), while in defensive transitions, compactness and counter-pressing help to either regain the ball, or regain the control of games. Players like Kylian Mbappé and Vinícius Jr. thrive in transition-to-attack-based setups due to their explosive pace and ability to create qualitative superiority in isolated situations. In defensive transition, teams can counter-press or reshape quickly to deny counter-attacks, producing defenders who can and must be able to defend initially past the halfway line and defend a space that may be greater than half a pitch!

Dynamic superiority is, therefore, not just an also-ran in the superiorities race; it is often the main horse. It is the skill that shows up that has the ability to take advantage of situations, whether in attack, in defence, or in either transition. It is the teams and players that display dynamic movement that worry coaches late at night!

Dutch coach and coach educator Raymond Verheijen talks a lot about the complexity involved in making 11 individual, thinking, idea-ridden brains all work together. A truly dynamic football team, whether under Guardiola or Diniz (or any other tactician), delivers a wonderful outcome of that.

> **TACTICAL TASK 48**
>
>
>
> HOW CAN YOU USE ELEMENTS OF DYNAMIC SUPERIORITY (MOVEMENT, FLUIDITY, ETC.) WITH INDIVIDUAL PLAYERS AND WITH YOUR UNITS AND TEAMS...
> 1. IN POSSESSION?
> 2. OUT OF POSSESSION?
> 3. IN TRANSITION?

Dynamic Pauses

Although a term that originated in Spain, the idea of 'la pausa' was put front and centre through the team tactics of Italian coach Roberto de Zerbi, due to the extremity of his version of the idea. It refers to the act of delaying a pass or action in order to manipulate the flow of the game and create a more favourable situation for the attacking team.

You will see it in its most obvious form when you see a centre-back in possession, studs on the ball, waiting for the opponent to press, before the team 'unpause' and destroy the press through pre-planned combinations. Far from being a passive hesitation, it is a deliberate, high-level tactical manoeuvre that allows players to exert control over time and space.

This momentary pause – sometimes prolonged or sometimes for just a split second – forces defenders to make decisions: press, hold their line, shift position, or cover a teammate. The true power of 'la pausa' lies in its capacity to disrupt the defensive structure of the opponent, making room for teammates to move into better positions or exploit newly created spaces. It's a hallmark of players with a high football IQ, those who see not just where players are, but where they *will* be. As a form of dynamic superiority (although it ironically starts with stillness!), the pause can be used to create or enhance different kinds of superiorities: numerical, positional, qualitative, and even collaborative.

More Ways to Be Better

From time to time, additional ideas and superiorities in football raise their head and are worth consideration. The brilliant thing about this game, as you will have seen throughout this book, is the flux of new ideas that change a sport woven into societies worldwide; a sport played formally and competitively virtually every day. You would imagine that the room for change is limited, yet the ideas keep coming!

I have briefly looked at other superiority ideas that have started gaining traction while conducting this book's deep dive research. Some of the ideas below are 'micro' ideas, elements of which you could probably assign to one of the other 'major' superiorities. However, taking superiorities and boxing them up is not the end goal here – finding advantages through the fusion of all superiorities in your team's games is the idea. In many ways, it might just be some of these minor ideas that help you be 1% better than those who may only be aware of up to five.

Temporal Superiority

Also known as 'speed-of-action superiority', it is temporary or momentary (to use a word we have used a lot throughout the book). This idea refers to executing specific one-off actions (or a succession of one-off actions) faster than the opponent can react.

This could be an individual action like a quick but high-quality executed pass, shot at goal, or a quick team passing sequence that rapidly disorganises the defence. We often see teams who are considerably weaker come up with a moment like this, resulting in a goal, for example.

Psychological Superiority

This is not only about your team being mentally stronger or more equipped than the opponent, it also involves influencing their mental state, causing them to lose confidence, make mistakes, or hesitate, for example.

This may come in the form of a high-pressing team forcing defenders into rushed clearances, bad decisions due to relentless pressure, or frustrating a talented attacking team with a low block. It might be capitalising on certain moments when they are mentally at a low ebb. We often use the term 'momentum' in football, which essentially means that one team is in this psychological ascendency. If we were to use a boxing analogy to bring this to life, this is where one fighter is striding forward – aggressive and throwing punches – compared to another retreating on the back foot.

Structural Superiority

This is when a team's overall formation and spacing create natural advantages when pitted against the other team's setup. It allows them to maintain control over the pitch, or force the opposition into focusing on your team and the problems you give them, rather than focusing on their game.

Football today is dominated by teams playing GK:4-3-2-1. Formations become popular for a reason – they provide a spread that essentially allows you to attack and defend in a balanced way. This, of course, will also depend on all the other superiorities. Playing a GK:3-5-2 as a base formation might be good for my team but not good for yours.

There are also disruptive formations. If most teams are playing in a similar way, and all other teams are thus familiar with this frequent problem, then offering another different problem might give you an edge. I would much rather play with a familiar, flat GK:4-3-3 formation than with a GK:3-5-1-1 with a diamond midfield, but I would also like to play against it more, too. Structural unfamiliarity has its benefits.

Conditional / Situational Superiority

This is the ability to create advantages based on often random, specific, game-by-game conditions. These would include such things as weather, pitch quality, or environmental considerations like fans, location, time of day, etc. In football, the term 'leveller' can be used to describe a random, unexpected condition that will help the qualitatively poor team compete with a stronger one.

This could include a physically strong team using wet conditions to their advantage by playing direct and forcing duels. Or a team using the enthusiasm and ferocity of their supporters to take advantage of a hostile atmosphere.

Refereeing Superiority

This is about taking advantage of randomly poor referee decisions (or even correct ones) that affect the game in ways you may not plan for. The full-back who gets a yellow card will find it extra tricky to commit to tackles in 1v1 situations, for example. If a team is playing with 10 players due to a sending-off, how can the opponent become dominant? Alternatively, if my team is reduced to 10 players, I may play in a way that is difficult for an opponent to break down. I once knew a coach who actively asserted that should his team ever be reduced to 10 players, they would be the best "man-down" team around – and they practised it. Being reduced to 10 players was, therefore, not an issue.

This idea, in particular, is quite controversial but has been a quiet part of the senior professional game for decades. It also refers to when a team is adept at influencing refereeing decisions through football actions like tactical fouling or simulation, or psychological manipulation like dropping hints in press conferences. It might even involve being over-friendly to officials before a game in the event that they might lend some sort of subjective favour during the game.

Conclusion

TACTICAL TASK 49

HOW CAN YOU USE THESE EXTRA SUPERIORITIES WITH YOUR TEAM?

Conclusion

Review & Final Task

When I included the below image on these pages, much earlier in this book, chances are it will have meant somewhat less to you than it does now.

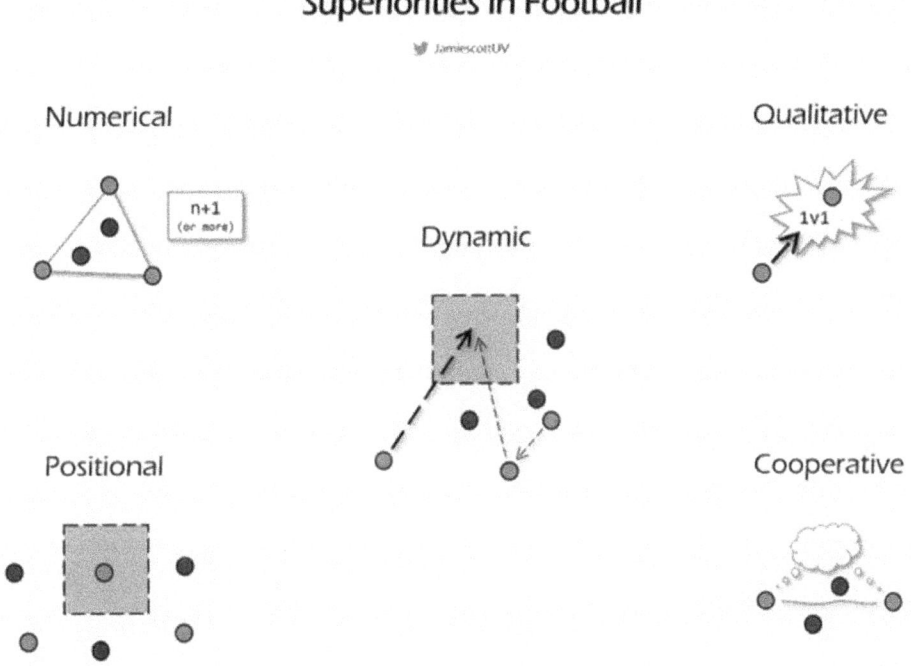

Throughout the book, we have journeyed and explored football tactics through the lens of superiorities. As a reader and a coach, your biggest challenge and outcome from each chapter is to consider how *you* might rethink how *you* perceive, plan, and execute *your* footballing philosophies.

Although we can analyse them all in detail individually, these five superiorities – Numerical, Qualitative, Positional, Cooperative, and Dynamic – are not stand-alone concepts. They are interdependent forces in the ever-shifting variability of a football match. This final chapter reinforces their definitions and their central concepts, and – more crucially – their integrations.

Numerical Superiority: More Than Just the Numbers

"More of us than you" may seem the simplest advantage to grasp, yet it demands the most strategic orchestration. From Bielsa's (+1)-(=)-(-1) system to transitional overloads and rest-defence structures, numerical superiority is never just about having more – it is about *where*, *when*, and *why* we have more players than you.

Coaches must think in pitch zones, phases, and moments, asking: "Are we numbers up in the build-up phase? Can we shift numbers dynamically to overload the final third?" etc. "Can we keep our +1 in zone X without compromising our balance elsewhere?"

Qualitative Superiority: Better Players, Better Choices

Having "better players" sounds obvious until you need to define *what better means*. Is it technical brilliance? Tactical intelligence? Psychological resilience? Physical advantage in some way? Or simply matchup suitability?

Qualitative superiority becomes most effective when your best players are positioned to face their opponents in the most favourable conditions. José Mourinho's infamous "Messi cage" is a perfect reminder: sometimes certain qualities need help from the other superiorities. The trick isn't always having the 'best' player, units, or teams but understanding how, when, and where to use them, individually or together – and against whom.

Positional Superiority: Right Place, Right Time

With your players on the pitch, in relation to BOTS – ball, opponents, teammates, and space – can they create positional advantages for individual players, units and teams?

Adding dynamic elements to positional superiority is even better – that is, players moving into high-value positions. Such positions may form fixed areas of the pitch – Zone 14, the halfspace, the golden zone, or the wide channels inside the penalty area. Or they may be more malleable spaces that change, depending on the positioning of players – behind the back line, between the lines, and all the other temporary spaces that open and close as the game evolves.

Cooperative Superiority: Better Together

Even when we don't have more players, or better ones, or even better positions, if we move, think, and act as a cohesive unit, groups of players can dominate and achieve an advantage. We see this across the professional game time and time again!

Cooperative superiority is often intangible – we are talking about team chemistry in a social sense, yes, but also in a tactical, game-understanding capacity. It's the familiarity and comfort of knowing your teammate's next action before they take it, or more comprehensively, it is all players knowing the habits of all their teammates and being able to relate that to their game strategy.

This superiority is deeply tied to clarity of roles, repetition, and trust – and simply playing together, training together and becoming familiar with the games of teammates. This could be anything from Messi knowing instinctively where Jordi Alba will run, or Haaland understanding where de Bruyne will pass – and building on those individuals through units and the full team.

Dynamic Superiority: The Master Superiority

Dynamic superiority interweaves with all other forms of superiority in the game. At its core, it refers to the ability of players or teams to create and exploit advantageous situations through intelligent, fluid movement, and adaptability during different moments of the game. This includes in-possession play, defensive organisation, and transitional phases. It even includes moments of stillness.

Diverse tactical systems can be built on the foundation of dynamic superiority. Positional Play, popularised by Pep Guardiola, relies on structured movement within fixed zones, while Relationism, as practised by Fernando Diniz, thrives on fluid interactions and intuitive decision-making based on the evolving context of the game. Both approaches depend heavily on player movement, either prescribed or instinctive, to unbalance opponents and create attacking opportunities.

Dynamic superiority is not limited to attacking phases. Defensively, teams also use movement to adapt their shape, press intelligently, and execute transitional strategies. High pressing, hybrid marking, and rest-defence principles are rooted in dynamic responses to BOTS. Teams like Real Madrid and Manchester City exemplify how transitions, both attacking and defensive, rely on pace, positioning, and intelligent spatial control to dominate.

Ultimately, dynamic superiority is not a supporting tactic but a central theme that enables all other superiorities.

Conclusion

This book has not been about giving you the "right answers." Not entirely, at least. Amongst all the information and examples, it has been about giving you the right questions and the tools to ask of yourself, including the 49 tasks throughout (Task 50 is below!).

If you have not completed all the tasks, it would be worth doing them now while the information is still reasonably fresh in your mind. If you have completed these tasks as you read, or somewhere in between, it would be well worth glancing through them again to reinforce learning. Maybe there is something else you learned or considered that you can add to your original ideas. After all, getting your teeth into improvements like this will only help you develop your coaching and help your players improve as a team.

Whether you coach grassroots players or elite professionals, your ability to create, identify, and exploit these superiorities will often define your success, so understanding them and how they apply to your team and players is important. Harness these superiorities not as abstract ideas, but as practical, trainable, repeatable advantages that can be achieved step by step.

TACTICAL TASK 50

USE THE ABOVE CONCLUDING CHAPTER TO REFRESH YOUR IDEAS ABOUT ALL THE SUPERIORITIES IN THE BOOK. WHICH IDEA OR SUPERIORITY WILL:

- **YOU START WITH?**
- **WANT TO LEARN MORE ABOUT?**
- **FOCUS ON MOST WITH YOU TEAM?**

Other Books from the Publisher

Some of our other 35+ soccer coaching books

www.BennionKearny.com/soccer

The Bearded Coach's Football Session Planner

"I have always struggled with session planners. They never include the sections I need, or the space to write and draw what I want."

Football coach and coach educator Peter Prickett was frustrated with existing planners, so he decided to develop his own. Created for grassroots football coaches right through to professionals alike, it is structured around Peter's insights and knowledge of best practice, and addresses key session aims, including: What structure am I going to use for this session? What questions will I ask of my players? How can I challenge the whole group, units, and individuals?

Incorporating detailed guidance on how to get the most out of the planner (including context, principles of play, intervention methods, session format, and more), alongside example plans to help kickstart planning, 40 blank templates are provided for you to create your own sessions. This A4 soft-cover planner uses high-quality paper and a wire-bound binding so it can be folded flat, and each template comprises two facing pages, creating an A3 working area, so the whole session can be viewed – in detail – at once.

Whether you are an occasional coach or developing teams full-time, *The Bearded Coach's Football Session Planner* is a vital tool in your armoury for delivering high-quality training sessions.

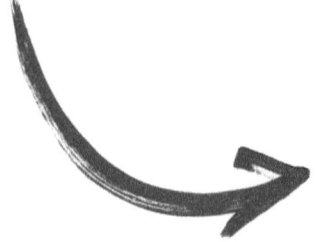

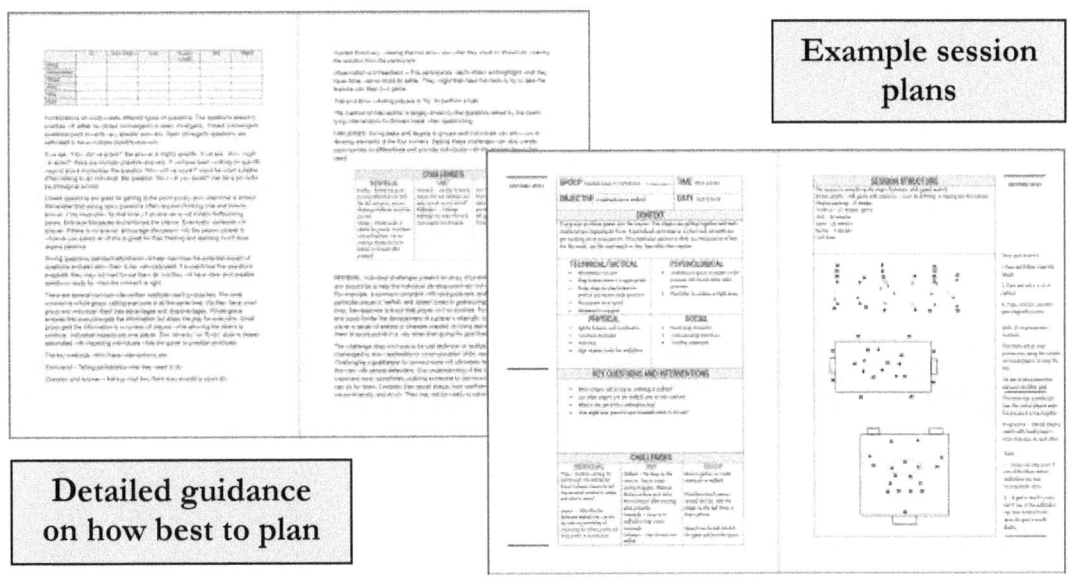

Example session plans

Detailed guidance on how best to plan

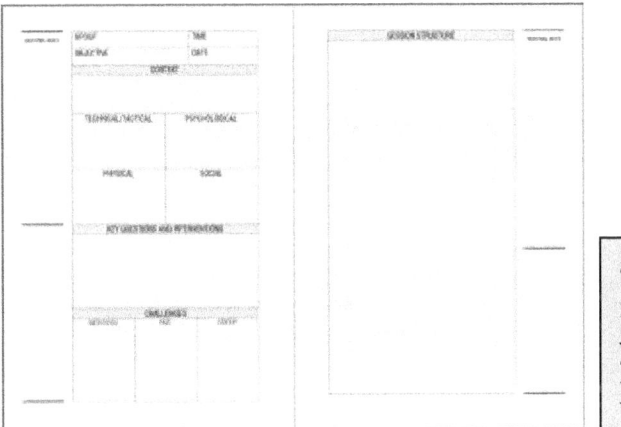

40 blank templates for you to create your training session plans

Peter Pricket is the author of the international bestsellers *Football's Principles of Play* and the *3v3 Coaching* books.

www.ingramcontent.com/pod-product-compliance
Lightning Source LLC
Chambersburg PA
CBHW060937170426
43194CB00027B/2978